Gizzi's
Healthy Appetite

Gizzi's
Healthy Appetite

Food to nourish the body and feed the soul

GIZZI ERSKINE

MITCHELL BEAZLEY

CONTENTS

INTRODUCTION   7

MY ETHOS   8

THE MODERN KITCHEN   12

1   SLURP   14

2   CRUNCH   32

3   CRISP   62

4   OOZE   80

5   CHAR   100

6   SOOTHE   118

7   SAVOUR   146

8   SPICE   166

9   SWEET   188

10 BASICS   210

    INDEX   220

    ACKNOWLEDGEMENTS   224

INTRODUCTION

There's no denying that I have a healthy appetite. I *love* food, I *love* eating and I *love* cooking. There's nothing I don't like to eat, except perhaps mangetout (pointless and flabby) and durian (poo fruit). I am a chef for two reasons: partly because I have a huge ego and I love feeding people and receiving their praise, but mainly because food makes people happy and has a way of soothing us from the inside out. Food doesn't just feed my body; it also feeds my soul.

I've written about healthy eating over the years, but recently I've seen an influx of books encouraging us to 'eat clean', make better choices, become vegan for our health or undertake extreme diets – and no one knows what the best advice actually is.

The more I see of people's food concerns on Twitter and Instagram, the more I see the love pouring out of food. It's as though people are so concerned about what they are putting into their bodies that food has lost its soul. Food should first and foremost be delicious. If we stick to some simple rules like eating a variety of different-coloured fruits and vegetables daily, eating smaller portions of better carbs, high-quality proteins and some good fats, then we will be getting all the nutrition we need for optimum health.

Back when I made *Cook Yourself Thin* we were using vegetables in place of carbohydrates, choosing non-starchy carbs as mash and putting vegetables in cakes to reduce the sugar and fat content. Now, there are some brilliant, new techniques for making things like vegan, gluten-free and sugar-free cakes, cauliflower rice and spiralized vegetable noodles, all of which can be a revelation when used in the right way with the right ingredients.

Cooking for a healthy appetite often seems to be geared more towards the healthy and less towards an appetite for food. However, I want to show you how to use those 'healthy' ingredients in a more delicious way. I also want to instil the message that being healthy is as much about moderation as it is about nutrition. I've always lived by the 80/20 rule: if you eat healthily 80 per cent of the time then you're allowed a little bit of something that may be considered 'naughty' the rest of the time.

The chapters of this book are divided into textures and flavours. For me, those textures and flavours often reflect my mood. For example, if I crave something braised or oozy it may mean that I'm after something rib-sticking and comforting but if I want crunch or crispness then I probably feel the need for something clean and fresh. Sometimes I want fiery food, so we have a chapter for spice, and other times I just need something sweet, and there's a chapter for that too.

So, here I am. I want to start a new food revolution; one where people have a better understanding of nutrition but don't forget that eating should be enjoyable.

MY ETHOS

Every week, when I open up a newspaper or women's magazine there's a new bit of health information that puts a spanner in the works of what I had previously thought was the right way to be healthy. So here is my ethos, and a bit about how I feel about food trends and what we can learn from them.

Firstly, I believe that having a better understanding of nutrition is not just about making your body healthier, it can also make you a better cook. The more I learn about different ingredients or come across a new cooking technique, vegetable or cut of meat, the more inspired I tend to be. I want this book to teach you that it's good to love food in all its guises and that sometimes your body needs to be fed what it's craving. Ultimately, I want people who are reading this book to try new things and push themselves into new areas of food, be it going to your local Asian supermarket or having a go at cooking with a new ingredient or gadget. I just hope people are inspired to cook fresh food using good ingredients.

THE 80/20 RULE

I follow the 80/20 rule. I'm good most of the time but absolutely allow myself to eat what I want the rest of the time, just so long as the food's been made with fresh ingredients. That said, I'm partial to a bit of processed cheese in my hamburger and I am going to eat it once every so often – so sue me! The 80/20 rule can be applied daily, but I think it works best when you eat healthily during the week and have a blow-out one day of the weekend and perhaps the odd dinner out. There's also another way you can apply the 80/20 rule: have 20 per cent less food on your plate, eat 20 per cent fewer carbohydrates and eat 20 per cent more vegetables. This will allow you to eat pretty much what you want, but you will be consuming 300–400 fewer calories a day. It's a simple but good rule to stick to.

CARBS

The glycaemic index (GI) scale shows how quickly blood sugar levels are raised after eating particular foods. Things like protein and green veg barely register on the scale, making them very low GI, and whole grains are also low GI because your body has to fight to digest them. Whereas, sugars, many fruits and processed white carbohydrates will make your blood sugar levels shoot up, releasing insulin into the blood and allowing the body to lay down fat. Because of this, I try to eat foods that are low GI whenever I can.

I'm pro carbs but I do think its important not to eat too many of them. We should be averaging (depending on gender and height) about 60–100g (in weight) of carbohydrate per meal, which, shockingly, is just a small bowl of pasta, an open sandwich or a handful of rice. Start weighing your carbs and you'll soon see that you eat more than you should. My theory is that it's better to eat some carbs than none.

SUGAR

It's a sad fact that if we eat a balanced diet of carbohydrates, dairy, protein, fruit and vegetables then we are already consuming the right amount of sugar for our bodies – and those who eat lots of carbs and fruit may be consuming too much sugar. This means that the addition of refined sugar into our diet can play havoc with our blood sugar levels. Just so long as we don't go crazy, a small amount of cake, chocolate or sweets isn't going to affect us *that* badly, but it's definitely something we should be aware of.

When you process sugar you remove the small amount of fibre that allows your body to absorb the sugar straight into the bloodstream. While there are lots of great-tasting unrefined sugars available, not many of them work in the same way that refined cane sugar does in cooking, which is a right royal pain in the ass. If you simply want to add some sweetness to something, that's fine, but if you're trying to make a meringue, cake or brownie, things can go horribly wrong. Trust me, I've done an absurd amount of tests trying to make this work so you don't have to. I have written most of my recipes using golden caster sugar (or muscovado sugar or maple syrup for flavour or caramelization). You can, if you like, use other sugars in any recipes that aren't for meringues, cakes or brownies. My favourite alternatives are coconut blossom nectar, coconut sugar, agave nectar and rapadura sugar. You may need to experiment with them as they all have varying degrees of sweetness.

FAT

Fat is back! We've known for ages that we should be eating good vegetable oils, such as olive, rapeseed, avocado, and fish oils because they contain a mixture of omega fatty acids and vitamin E. Now, we also have coconut oil, which despite being a saturated fat is brilliant for metabolizing fat. And the best news of all is that butter is okay again and ghee is even better! In fact, it now seems that butter is not just okay for you, it's as good for you as any other fat.

So what went wrong? In the late 1950s a study was released that showed countries that ate more fat had higher rates of heart disease so government guidelines told people to eat less saturated fat (including butter). Since then more research has been done to show that it isn't as simple as that and you need both fat and cholesterol in your diet. Fat does not make you fat. Butter and ghee contain good fats and vitamins that lower your risk of a heart attack compared to margarine. Butter makes veg taste awesome due to fat-soluble vitamins in the veg, and ghee is better than vegetable oil for cooking as it is more stable at high temperatures.

My advice is to use a mixture of all of these different oils, eat 2-3 portions of oily fish a week as well as eating nuts, seeds and avocados. Just because all of these things have the potential to make you fat doesn't mean you don't need them in your diet in order to make your body work.

MEAT

If there is one thing that you take away from this book, let it be this: eat better protein and eat less of it. It is easy to overeat everything (carbs, fat, sugar, booze and meat) and this has an effect on our bodies. However, eating too much meat also has an effect on the environment. The way we're going, it is looking increasingly likely that we will not be able to continue to consume meat the way we do today. We should be eating less meat, and the meat we eat should be better quality.

I always recommend buying meat from a butcher and using small producers who rear animals ethically and butcher in a more skilled way. This is my only mega-snobbery and it's also about animal welfare and the environment. I'm not pushing organic, I just want you to buy the best meat you can afford.

VEGETABLES

Vegetables (and fruits) are full of micronutrients. In most cases we get more nutrients into our system if food is eaten raw, so eat tons of raw veg, fruits and salads. Green juices are a great way to absorb these nutrients into the body quickly, but I think these juices should be a supplement not a substitute for food. Most green veg are alkalizing and help us maintain a better pH in our bodies, which is why everyone is going greens crazy – keep up this trend. 'An avocado a day keeps the wrinkles at bay' is my new theory and 'eat more veg' is my motto. So play around with vegetables: roast them, mash them, spiralize them, rice them, juice them and make salads – just make sure over 50 per cent of your daily food intake is made up of eating them.

DAIRY

If you really and truly have a dairy intolerance, avoid soya milk because a lot of it is made from GM crops, it's highly processed and it's just not very tasty. Go for cold-pressed almond milks (I love the stuff from The Pressery) as they are without doubt the tastiest, though I have also tasted some delicious hazelnut and macadamia nut milks.

STOCK

I've always used fresh stock in my food and have preached about it from the hilltops. Why on earth would you cook fresh food and then ram a sodium-filled stock cube into it? It's the biggest oxymoron in cooking. Fresh is always best when it comes to stock: for flavour, for clarity and also for its gelatinous and health-giving properties. Marrowbones are super for you, and bone broth or stock is full of calcium and collagen and is also hydrating and anti-inflammatory. If you want a glossy, restaurant-quality gravy or sauce, fresh stock will reduce to a perfectly flavoured, lip-smacking consistency.

THE MODERN KITCHEN

This new way of cooking may require some new equipment. Here's my list of kitchen must-haves:

A good knife and chopping board

These two things can be expensive, despite them being at the heart of almost every dish. Yes, you can go and grab yourself a knife and board from the supermarket but that will hold you back a bit as a cook. The way I see it, a good knife is for life, whereas the cheaper ones need replacing every 2-3 years. I buy Kin knives for value or go to the Japanese Knife Company if I want to splurge. The same ethos is true for a board. A wooden chopping board will last forever (just look at butchers' blocks) but plastic or glass will need replacing – and don't get me started on how they ruin your knives.

Nonstick pans

Cooking with a nonstick pan means that you need less oil, so they are essential if you're trying to cook with less fat. Go for a really heavy-based one – I love the toughened nonstick pans from Le Creuset.

A griddle pan

An essential pan for modern cooking, and I use mine at least three times a week. The griddle lines add caramelization and barbecue flavour to meat, fish, vegetables or bread. I like a griddle pan with wider ridges as the thinner ones can make your food taste a little too barbecued. Always buy a really heavy cast-iron griddle pan as the lighter ones don't add the flavour you need and fall to bits.

A really good casserole

I couldn't live without my cast-iron casserole dishes. They are more important to me than almost any other kitchen equipment. The last couple of years has seen the rise of the slow cooker, but no slow cooker can do what a lidded, cast-iron casserole can do, be it on the hob or in a low oven. For slow cooking, a really good casserole is unbeatable.

Tons of mixing bowls
Ideally, you should have a mixture of glass and metal bowls in a variety of sizes to meet every kitchen eventuality.

Electric weighing scales
Scales are essential to make sure you're not eating too much. Over-consuming is such a common problem that it's worth getting into the boring habit of weighing out your food, especially carbohydrates. I prefer electric scales as they are more precise.

A spiralizer
A spiralizer is a great way to cut back on carbs and eat more fresh vegetables and it's really worth the money (the Hemsley+Hemsley spiralizer is one of the best I've tried). If you can't afford one, a hand-held vegetable ribboner will do the same thing and you'll build muscles in the process.

A powerful blender
A pretty kitchen blender just won't do in my eyes. It's more important to consider the power of a blender: the higher the power, the finer the blend. Vitamix blenders are the best, blitzing smoothies, soups and pastes to oblivion, but are very expensive so buy the best you can afford.

A food processor
I use a food processor almost every day, for everything from making pastes to cauliflower rice.

A stand mixer
This is a gadget that's on most people's kitchen wish lists. You need a stand mixer to whisk, beat or knead food so it's a baking gadget. I lived with my KitchenAid for years but got an Electrolux Grand Cuisine stand mixer this year and it's been a game-changer. If a mixer is too pricey, use an electric hand whisk for whisking and beating.

SLURP

....

SMOOTHIES, SOUPS & NOODLES

BANANA, DATE, ALMOND MILK & BEE POLLEN SMOOTHIE

My friend Elly, who owns the Pear Café in Bristol, is a genius when it comes to healthy cooking. She has been doing the 5:2 diet for a couple of years and has not only lost a couple of stone but also created some of the most brilliant recipes. Her knowledge of ingredients is second to none. When we were hanging out in Spain, she introduced me to bee pollen because I get terrible hayfever and have the worst allergic reaction to insect bites — and the bee pollen genuinely helped. That is what bee pollen is best known for but it also does a multitude of other things: it boosts energy, smoothes the skin, is an anti-inflammatory for the respiratory system, has enzymes to aid digestion and helps the cardiovascular system. It really is a superfood. I drink one of these smoothies in the morning and it kicks me up the butt. I feel better for doing so and I swear my hayfever has gone away.

....

As with any smoothie recipe, it's all about the blender. I like to use the most powerful blender available (see page 13).

Place the ingredients into a blender in the order stated and blitz for 1 minute if you have a powerful blender or 1 minute 20 seconds if your blender is the classic type. Pour into glasses and serve.

2 bananas (the ripest you can find as they are sweetest), peeled, cut into chunks and frozen
6 soft pitted dates (the best quality you can afford)
1 tablespoon bee pollen
500ml really good pressed almond milk

SUPER GREEN SMOOTHIE

Everybody's doing it, so you might as well do it as well. This is the power juice of all power juices and it will give you the biggest spring in your step you could ever want. Any good blender will do. The apples and pears will add tons of sweetness and be the liquid in the smoothie; the kale is alkaline, which will balance your pH levels; the avocado has vitamin E and good oils that help burn fat and will make you look radiant; and the herbs provide an abundance of antioxidants. Drink this for breakfast with a handful of almonds to give yourself a protein boost. You will be bouncing off the walls before you know it!

Juice the apples and pears.

Next, place the rest of the ingredients in a blender in the order they are listed along with the juices. Blend for 1 minute, or until totally smooth: the kale can take a while to blend. Once it is smooth, divide between 2 tall glasses and serve with a straw.

4 Granny Smith apples
5 pears
juice of 1 lemon
1 kiwifruit, peeled and frozen
   in chunks
1 avocado, peeled, stoned and
   chopped
1 tablespoon pea or hemp
   protein (optional)
a good handful of green kale,
   trimmed of its stems and
   chopped
a good handful of mint
a good handful of parsley

PREPARATION TIME
15 minutes, plus standing
and chilling

COOKING TIME None

CHILLED CUCUMBER, AVOCADO & BUTTERMILK SOUP

Chilled soups are one of the greatest things about summer. This is a really simple one made with buttermilk, which has a slight tang, alongside cucumber, avocado, dill and mint. The cucumber is the base flavour; the avocado is mainly there for texture, making the soup silky; and the dill and mint just add freshness. Make it in the morning and allow to homogenize for a few hours in the fridge, then eat for a late summer lunch when the soup's extra cold, adding a few ice cubes if you like.

....

Coarsely chop 5 of the cucumber halves and transfer to a large bowl. Add the buttermilk, lemon juice, spring onions, dill, mint, garlic and salt and pepper. Stir to combine, cover with cling film and leave to stand at room temperature for 1 hour to blend the flavours. Dice the remaining cucumber half and set aside until ready to serve.

In a powerful blender, purée the cucumber mixture together with the avocado until smooth. With the machine running, slowly add the stock and purée until it is fully incorporated; this will take about 30 seconds. Transfer to a jug, cover with cling film and refrigerate for about 2 hours, or until chilled.

Pour the soup into bowls, then top with the chopped cucumber, drizzle with the oil and a little extra buttermilk. Garnish with the extra mint and dill and serve immediately.

3 cucumbers, halved lengthways
   and deseeded
250ml buttermilk, plus extra
   to serve
2 tablespoons lemon juice
2 spring onions, (green and
   white parts, chopped
3 tablespoons chopped dill,
   plus extra to garnish
a few mint leaves, plus extra
   tiny mint leaves to garnish
1 small garlic clove, chopped
1 large ripe but firm avocado,
   peeled and stoned
420ml fresh White Chicken or
   Veggie Stock (see pages
   212–13), chilled
2 tablespoons really good,
   fruity extra virgin olive oil
sea salt flakes and white pepper

PREPARATION TIME
25 minutes, plus chilling

COOKING TIME
30 minutes

CHLODNIK
(CHILLED POLISH BEETROOT SOUP WITH DILL PICKLES, EGG & PRAWNS)

As far as chilled soups go, chlodnik has to be one of the unsung heroes. It's basically borscht that is enriched with buttermilk and soured cream and topped with an array of jazzy things like peeled prawns, boiled eggs, gherkins and mounds of dill. With her Polish heritage, my mum always waxed lyrical about buying bottles of borscht as a teen and pimping it up with way too much soured cream, making it look a little like Pepto-Bismol! She has a point but this soup tastes anything but. Making this soup is a really great way to use up a glut of beetroot in the winter, freeze and then turn into a terrific dish in the summer.

....

Heat the oil in a large saucepan. Add the onion and cook over a low heat for about 10 minutes, or until translucent and softened enough that you can squish through the onion with your fingertips. Add the beetroot and cucumber and cook for 10 minutes, or until the beetroot starts to break down. Pour in the stock and cook at an aggressive simmer for a further 10 minutes, or until the beetroot is really soft.

Remove from the heat and stir in the buttermilk and soured cream. Using either a blender or immersion blender, blitz the soup for about a minute, or until it's completely smooth: it should be the thickness of single cream. You can strain the soup at this point if you like it extra smooth (I do!). Season with salt and pepper and the pickle brine and leave to cool, then pop it in the fridge to chill for at least 5 hours. I always like to put the soup in the freezer for 30 minutes before serving to get it really chilled.

Ladle the soup into bowls and top each bowl of soup with 3 of the egg quarters. Add some gherkins, prawns and dill before serving with extra buttermilk drizzled with olive oil.

1 tablespoon olive oil, plus extra to serve
1 onion, finely chopped
4 beetroot, peeled and grated
1 Lebanese cucumber or ½ regular cucumber, peeled and grated
600ml fresh White Chicken or Veggie Stock (see pages 212–13)
500ml buttermilk. plus extra to serve
500ml soured cream
3 tablespoons dill pickle brine
sea salt flakes and freshly ground black pepper

To serve

5 free-range eggs, hard-boiled and cut into quarters
2 dill pickles, chopped
200g cooked, peeled small prawns (I prefer Atlantic 'shell-on' baby prawns, peeled)
a small bunch of dill, roughly chopped

MULLIGATAWNY SOUP WITH POACHED EGGS & CRISPY SHALLOTS

Mulligatawny is an Anglo-Indian soup that is curried and thickened with lentils or rice – sometimes with meat, sometimes without. My version is a chicken-based soup that's spiced and thickened with lentils, but I've made more of a meal out of it with a soft-poached egg perched on the top and some crispy shallots. I make a batch of this soup for dinner on a Sunday night and serve it this way, then serve it with chopped-up boiled eggs the next day when I'm at work. Everyone is jealous of me when I have this lunch – it's epic.

···

3 tablespoons ghee or vegetable oil
6 free-range chicken thighs, skin on, bone in
1 large onion, finely chopped
6 garlic cloves, finely chopped
½ green chilli
3cm piece of fresh root ginger, peeled and grated
1½ tablespoons ground cumin
1 tablespoon ground coriander
1 teaspoon ground turmeric
½ teaspoon cumin seeds
½ teaspoon coriander seeds
½ teaspoon black mustard seeds
2 dried chillies
200g red lentils
2 litres fresh White Chicken or Veggie Stock (see pages 212–13)
200ml coconut milk
juice of ¼ lemon
a small bunch of fresh coriander, roughly chopped
sea salt flakes and freshly ground black pepper

For the garnish

4 free-range eggs, poached (I use Cotswold Legbar eggs as they have orange yolks)
natural yogurt
Crispy Shallots (see page 79)

Heat 2 tablespoons of the ghee or vegetable oil in a deep saucepan over a medium-high heat. Season the chicken pieces with salt and pepper and then fry them in batches until browned all over. Remove the chicken with a slotted spoon and set aside.

Meanwhile, place the onion, garlic, chilli, ginger and ground spices in a food processor and blitz to make a curry paste.

Once all the chicken is browned, add the remaining ghee or vegetable oil to the pan and fry the whole spices for 1 minute, or until they start to pop. Add the curry paste and cook slowly for 5 minutes or until the paste is less 'wet' and has started to tinge golden. Add the lentils, stock and coconut milk and return the chicken to the pan. Cook for 45 minutes, or until the chicken is cooked through and easily peeled from the bone and the lentils are completely soft.

Using tongs, remove the chicken from the pan and set aside. When it is cool enough to handle remove the skin and use 2 forks to shred the meat off the bone (one fork to hold the chicken steady and the other to tear the meat apart).

In the meantime, keep cooking the soup until the liquid has reduced by about 1cm and the stock has become rich and full of flavour, then season with plenty of salt and pepper. Return the shredded chicken to the pan. Remove from the heat, add the lemon juice and half the coriander and check the seasoning. Serve immediately, each bowl of soup topped with a poached egg, a swirl of yogurt, some crispy shallots and more coriander.

SERVES 4
....

PREPARATION TIME
10 minutes

COOKING TIME
2–2½ hours

CHICKEN PHO WITH DAIKON NOODLES

After I'd caught the spiralizing bug, it was then a matter of seeing how it could be utilized. Spiralizing doesn't fit into every type of recipe, and it's wrong to just use it as a pasta or noodle substitute. The way to get the best out of spiralizing is to make the vegetable work for the dish – this pho is a great example of that as the daikon noodles complement the flavour of the classic Vietnamese broth. What you have here is a highly delicious, nutritious, health-giving, no-carb soup that can be eaten as a low-calorie lunch, or even as a snack through the day. What I tend to do is make the broth and save it in jars and put the spiralized daikon and all the accompaniments in a separate lunch bowl. This way when you get to work you can heat up the broth until it's piping hot and then serve it with all the bits. Less a game changer and more a life changer.

....

1 whole medium free-range chicken
400ml fresh White Chicken Stock (see page 212)
2 onions, roughly sliced
3cm piece of fresh root ginger, peeled and sliced
1 bulb of garlic, cut in half horizontally
6 black peppercorns
1 star anise
1 cinnamon stick
1 lemon grass stalk, bashed
1 teaspoon salt
2 tablespoons fish sauce, and maybe some extra for a final season
2 teaspoons palm sugar
2 daikon, about 400g

To serve

2 Thai red chillies, finely sliced
2–3 spring onions (green part only), finely sliced,
1 onion, very finely sliced into rings
a small handful of coriander
a few sprigs of Thai basil
a handful of bean sprouts
1 lime, cut into 8 wedges

You will also need a spiralizer

Put the chicken in a large casserole together with the stock, onions, ginger, garlic, peppercorns, star anise, cinnamon stick, lemon grass, salt, fish sauce and palm sugar, then top up with water until the chicken is covered. Bring to the boil, then reduce the heat and simmer for 1½ hours with the lid on, then take the chicken out and set aside to cool.

Strain the liquid from the cooking vegetables, and then pour the broth into a saucepan and reduce down for about 30 minutes until you have a rich chicken, flavoursome broth. You may need to season it with more fish sauce at this stage.

While the broth is reducing and when the chicken is cool enough to handle, shred the chicken and spiralize the daikon and set aside.

Place a quarter of the spiralized daikon into each soup bowl and top with the shredded chicken, chillies, spring onions, sliced onion, coriander, Thai basil and bean sprouts. Once you are happy with the flavour of the chicken broth, pour about 250ml into the bowls and leave for few minutes before serving with lime wedges.

SAMGYETANG
(GINSENG BABY CHICKEN SOUP)

Samgyetang is one of the purest dishes I've eaten and it's also one of the most health-giving dishes in Korean cookery as its main ingredient is ginseng. This soup is reminiscent of what I consider to be the best kind of cold-busting foods such as Jewish chicken noodle soup or Vietnamese Pho. Ginseng is expensive and can be hard to come by, though if you go to Chinatown or visit a Chinese doctor you will find it in abundance. If you find it hard to obtain ginseng, you can use a pinch of ginseng tea in the same way. To make this soup you stuff baby chickens with Korean rice and some aromatics and then poach them in a stock with more of the same aromatics. The rice cooks inside the chicken and the dish is ready when the chicken is falling off the bone. Serve the soup with a dipping salt and kimchi.

75g Korean or Japanese short
  grain rice
25g sprouted Korean mixed rice
  (if you can't get hold of this
  just increase the amount of
  short grain rice to 100g)
2 small free-range chickens
  (poussins)
3 small ginseng roots
5 ginkgo beans (optional)
a few jujubes (Korean or
  Chinese dates)
a few slices of fresh root
  ginger, peeled
8 garlic cloves
500ml White Chicken Stock
  (see page 212, the stock must
  be cold)
500ml water
6 spring onions, plus 2 very
  thinly sliced spring onions
  (green parts only)
Gizzi's Kimchi (see page 217),
  to serve

For the dipping salt

1 teaspoon salt
¼ teaspoon white pepper
¼ teaspoon black pepper
pinch of caster sugar

Soak both types of rice in a bowl of water for 1 hour.

  Strain the rice and stuff each chicken with half the rice, a ginseng root, a ginkgo bean, a jujube, a slice of ginger and 2 garlic cloves.

  Pop the stuffed chickens into a large cast-iron casserole dish. Pour over the stock and measurement water, and then add the remaining aromatics and the whole spring onions to the casserole. Simmer over a medium heat for 40–50 minutes, or until cooked through. The chickens don't have to be completely immersed in liquid as you are braising them and you want the soup to reduce a little so that it becomes richly flavoured by the end of the cooking time. When cooked properly, the chicken can be easily pulled apart by chopsticks.

  Meanwhile, make the dipping salt by mixing together all the ingredients in a small serving bowl or dipping bowl. Add half the dipping salt to the soup and stir. Transfer a chicken to each serving bowl, ladle over the soup and finish by sprinkling over the sliced spring onions. I like to dip the chicken into the dipping salt and serve the Kimchi in a small bowl alongside the soup.

SERVES 4
....

PREPARATION TIME
25 minutes

COOKING TIME
15 minutes

MUL NAENGMYEON
(COLD KOREAN NOODLE SALAD)

I first had this salad at a proper Korean barbecue restaurant in Korea on the island of Jeju. The most interesting thing about the dish was the salad that they served alongside. It was an ice-cold buckwheat noodle salad covered in a sticky, acidic but searingly spicy dressing accompanied by cucumber and boiled eggs. I've researched this recipe to death and although I tried it with pork, it is sometimes served with rare beef. The coolest thing about this dish is that it's served with ice-cold beef stock that chills the salad right down. It's a weird thing for a westerner but if you've ever had a bullshot (beef stock, vodka, Worcestershire sauce and Tabasco sauce) you will understand why this is a winner!

....

2cm thick piece of rump steak, about 400g
1 tablespoon cooking oil
200g buckwheat soba noodles
30g caster sugar
100ml rice wine vinegar
100g gochujang (Korean chilli paste)
2 tablespoons sesame oil
500ml fresh Beef Stock (see page 213), chilled
½ Korean pear or a really firm regular pear, julienned
¼ cucumber, julienned
¼ daikon, juilienned
2 spring onions, very finely sliced into rings
2 free-range eggs, hard boiled for 8 minutes, chilled and peeled
sea salt flakes and freshly ground black pepper
toasted sesame seeds, to sprinkle (I like a mixture of white and black)

Season the steak with salt and pepper. Heat a large frying pan until lightly smoking. Add the oil and then sear the steak for 1 minute on each side. You want the steak to be somewhere between blue and medium-rare but with some serious char on the outside. Remove from the pan and leave to rest while you get on with making the rest of the salad.

Bring a pan of water to the boil and season with plenty of salt. Add the noodles and cook for 1 minute less than the packet instructions. This will make sure the noodles are nice and al dente. Drain and refresh under cold running water, then pop into a bowl of iced water to chill them quickly. They need to be really cold.

Heat the sugar and vinegar in a small saucepan until the sugar dissolves and it becomes a light syrup. Whisk in the gochujang, then the sesame oil and remove from the heat. You now have your dressing.

Do not heat the stock. The point of this recipe is that the stock is served chilled. Pour the stock into 4 bowls. Add the noodles in a neat swirl – Korean food is all about presentation – and cover with 2½ tablespoons of the dressing.

Thinly slice the beef, place it to the side of the noodles and pour over the pan juices. Lay the cucumber, diakon and spring onion slices to the side of the beef, then place half an egg next to the salad. Finish by topping with more dressing, if needed, and a good sprinkling of sesame seeds.

PREPARATION TIME
25 minutes

COOKING TIME
15 minutes

TOM YUM GOONG
(HOT & SOUR FISH STEW)

1 tablespoon vegetable oil
1 lemon grass stick, very
   thinly sliced
4-5 thin slices of fresh root
   ginger
3-4 garlic cloves, thinly
   sliced
350g baby plum tomatoes, halved
400ml fresh White Chicken Stock
   (see page 212)
2 tablespoons lime juice
2-3 tablespoons fish sauce
5-7 kaffir lime leaves, thinly
   sliced
12 raw tiger prawns, peeled,
   deveined and cut quite deeply
   down the back
1 sea bream, filleted and each
   fillet cut into 4 lengthways
1 squid, gutted, slashed and
   cut into bite-sized pieces
sea salt flakes
a good handful of Thai holy
   basil
Crispy Shallots (see page 79),
   to garnish
coriander leaves, to garnish
banh cuon rice wrappers or rice
   noodles or rice, to serve

For the paste

3 shallots
3 lemon grass sticks, bashed
   and root removed
4cm piece of galangal (or fresh
   root ginger)
5 kaffir lime leaves, thinly
   sliced
6 Thai bird's eye chillies
1 teaspoon Thai roasted chilli
   paste or hot chilli powder
½ teaspoon dried shrimp paste
1 teaspoon palm or brown sugar
5 coriander roots

I bloody love tom yum goong, the hot and sour prawn soup from Thailand. There's also a similar dish from Cambodia called solmar machoor, which is a soupy fish stew that is as fiery as it is sour — this is my take on them both. All the legwork for this stew is in the paste and in cooking down the tomatoes, so it's really important that you take your time and do this slowly to encourage the natural sweetness you want from the dish. I've served the stew with something completely odd — Vietnamese banh cuon rice wrappers, which I've used like big, fat, wide noodles. If you can't find them, any Vietnamese rice noodle will do or you can even use rice, which is wicked to soak up the stew.

··

To make the paste, pound together all the ingredients to form a smoothish paste. I prefer to do this using a pestle and mortar, but this can be time-consuming so blitz the ingredients in a food processor or blender if you're in a rush.

Heat the oil in a large saucepan. Fry the lemon grass, ginger and garlic for 2 minutes. This is a little unconventional but it will give the stew a deeper, more caramelized flavour. Add 3 tablespoons of the prepared paste and fry for 1 minute, then add the tomatoes and cook for 3 minutes, or until they start to melt. Pour over the stock, lime juice, fish sauce, kaffir lime leaves and cook for 5 minutes. Add the prawns, fish and squid, season with salt and cook for 3-4 minutes, or until the seafood is just cooked and the prawns are pink. Stir through the holy basil and garnish with Crispy Shallots and coriander leaves. Serve the stew with flat rice wrappers, rice noodles or rice.

PIMPED-UP PAD THAI

PREPARATION TIME
20 minutes

COOKING TIME
10 minutes

½ tablespoon vegetable oil
50g strip of firm tofu (10cm
  long, 1cm wide and about
  8mm thick)
½ banana shallot, thinly sliced
5 raw king prawns, peeled and
  deeply deveined (I leave the
  tails on)
1 free-range egg
100g pad Thai noodles, soaked
  for 20 minutes, then drained
50ml fresh White Chicken Stock
  (see page 212)
5g salted radish, finely
  chopped (you can't substitute
  this, so just leave out if you
  can't find it)
50g bean sprouts
5 long garlic chives, each cut
  into 6 pieces

For the pad Thai sauce

1 tablespoon Sriracha chilli
  sauce
1 tablespoon palm or light
  muscovado sugar
3 tablespoons tamarind paste
  (made from rehydrating
  tamarind)
1 tablespoon oyster sauce
1 tablespoon fish sauce
½ teaspoon Maggi liquid
  seasoning (optional)

To serve

1 tablespoon chopped roasted
  peanuts
1 lime, halved
20g bean sprouts

Pad Thai is one of the more difficult noodle dishes to cook. It's not actually that hard but it's got some weird techniques that, if you're a Westerner, you may find a bit flummoxing. You need to fry the component parts separately and use a wok that is scarily hot. But if you have all of your ingredients at the ready, then this is one of the funnest and fastest ways to cook. So why is this pimped up? In my youth in Thailand I was taught to make it with ketchup and Maggi liquid seasoning (along with the obligatory tamarind and fish sauce). It's what all the kids were doing and it really made the whole sweet, sour, spicy balance work. I've since visited Thailand and been taught a new way to make it that has the same ethos as what I learnt in the Nineties, but packs even more of a punch as it uses California-made Sriracha Thai chilli sauce (instead of the ketchup) and oyster sauce, too. Maggi liquid seasoning contains MSG — use it if you want to.

....

Mix together all the ingredients for the pad Thai sauce in a bowl and set aside. You can make a bulk-load of this sauce and keep it in the fridge for up to a month if you like. I've given this sauce to people as presents: better than a box of chocolates if you ask me!

Heat the oil in a wok. When it's REALLY hot, add the strip of tofu and fry it on all sides, being careful not to move it around until it has caramelized and detached itself. Remove from the pan and drain on kitchen paper. Cut the strip of tofu into 15–20 slices.

Add the shallot to the wok and fry for 1 minute. Then add the king prawns and cook on both sides until they turn pink. Push the prawns to one side of the wok and crack in the egg. Quickly scramble the egg in large folds. Throw in the noodles, which will still be firm, then add the chicken stock and stir-fry for 2 minutes. Add the pad Thai sauce and stir-fry for 2 minutes. Return the tofu to the wok, add the salted radish, if using, bean sprouts and garlic chives and stir-fry for 1 minute more. Serve on a plate with the chopped peanuts, lime and extra bean sprouts.

CRUNCH

SALADS & RAW VEG

SERVES 4
....

PREPARATION TIME
5 minutes

COOKING TIME
20 minutes

KALE CHIPS

The first time that I was given kale chips was in a health food shop in Los Angeles where the dehydrated chips were freshly made. I was impressed by how delicious they were, but it wasn't until I tried them baked that I really grasped how good they could be. Kale is one of the best body alkalizers you can get your hands on and it also tastes wonderful. The great thing about kale chips is that they are low carb but taste really naughty, like actual crisps, because even a tiny bit of oil will make them crisp up. When you take these out of the oven they will be a little bit soft but in a matter of minutes they will be as crisp as any crisp could be and equally as moreish, while also packing a nutritional punch! I've seasoned these simply with nutritional yeast and salt, which gives them a marmitey and almost meaty finish, and the nutritional yeast is full of B vitamins.

....

Heat the oven to 150°C/Gas Mark 2. Line 2 large baking trays with parchment paper.

Remove the leaves from the stems of the kale and roughly tear up the leaves into large pieces. (You can compost the stems or freeze them to use in smoothies.) Wash and thoroughly dry the leaves.

Place the kale leaves in a large bowl and massage the oil into all the nooks and crannies of the leaves until they are thoroughly coated. Now sprinkle with the salt and nutritional yeast. Spread the kale out over the prepared baking trays in a single layer, being careful not to overcrowd with the kale.

Bake for 10 minutes, then rotate the trays and bake for a further 5–10 minutes, or until the kale begins to firm up and shrink a little. Leave the kale to cool on the baking trays for 3 minutes, or until it crisps up. The chips will last for about 2 weeks in a sealed plastic container. You can eat about 50g of kale crisps per day.

200g kale
1 tablespoon olive oil
pinch of salt
1 tablespoon nutritional yeast
  (optional – but the chips do
  taste better with it)

....

SERVES 6
....

PREPARATION TIME
15 minutes

COOKING TIME
None

CRUDITÉS

My dream crudités

1 small Lebanese cucumber
   or ½ regular cucumber,
   deseeded and cut into batons
6 radishes with leaves
4 baby carrots
4 cauliflower florets
4 purple cauliflower florets
4 romesco cauliflower florets
4 celery stick tops with leaves
4 asparagus spears, blanched
   for a few seconds and
   refreshed in iced water
4 Little Gem lettuce leaves
4 chicory leaves

Crudités can feel so bloody Eighties bad buffet party, but when done well it is one of the most beautiful and delicious ways to show off really great vegetables. A platter overflowing with an array of crunchy vegetables in different colours and shapes looks best, but sometimes simply serving some beautiful radishes, for example, can suffice as it's the dips as much as the veg that do the talking. Here are three of my favourite ways (see pages 36–9) to show off crudités. The crudités can be a mixture of any salad vegetables you have to hand, but I've listed my favourites here.

Arrange your crudités neatly on a serving plate and serve with dipping sauces (see pages 36–9).

SERVES 2 as a snack, part of a lunch
or starter with enough dip for 6

PREPARATION TIME
10 minutes

COOKING TIME
None

SOPHIE'S ANCHOVY DIP

The crudités and dip that my friend Sophie Michell serves at her restaurant, Pont St, are the best I've had outside of the south of France. Eat them as a snack, as lunch alongside some cured meat or as a starter.

2 garlic cloves, grated
1 tablespoon Dijon mustard
3–4 anchovies in oil, bashed
   into a purée
1 tablespoon sherry or white
   wine vinegar
squeeze of lemon juice
2 free-range egg yolks
150ml olive oil
75ml vegetable oil
sea salt flakes and freshly
   ground black pepper

Pop the garlic, mustard and anchovy purée into a mixing bowl with plenty of salt and pepper. Add the vinegar, lemon juice and egg yolks, and then use a small whisk to whisk them together. Slowly whisk in the oils, adding them in a slow thin stream, as if you were making mayonnaise, in order for the sauce to emulsify. If the oil is added too quickly the sauce will either split or not thicken properly. Check the seasoning, and then transfer to a dipping bowl. Keep in the fridge for up to 1 week.

SERVES 6
....

PREPARATION TIME
10 minutes, plus soaking

COOKING TIME
None

SMOKED SALMON & CODS' ROE

This is my favourite way to eat crudités. This dip is also my cat Kimchi's favourite human food. It's basically taramosalata that's been pimped up with smoked salmon to become lighter and a little more moussey, and it's great as a snack served with radishes or crispy fish skin. The method is similar to making a mayonnaise but much easier. Cooking with cods' roe may be a new one for you, but if you like shop-bought taramosalata then you will love the freshness of making it from scratch yourself.

....

Before you start, soak the cods' roe in a bowl of cold water for at least a couple of hours. Drain it thoroughly, and then peel off the skin.

Put the cods' roe in a blender with the garlic and blend it at top speed, gradually pouring in the lemon juice. Start adding the oils a drop at a time (as you would if you were making mayonnaise) and keep adding the oil until the mixture becomes firm. Add the smoked salmon and blend. Pour in the boiling water or just enough to blend until the mixture becomes a soft mousse. Don't add the water before the mixture has become solid or it will separate. Sprinkle with black onion seeds and serve alongside radishes or mixed Crudités.

225g smoked cods' roe
1 garlic clove, grated
3 tablespoons lemon juice
150ml light olive oil
250ml vegetable oil
50–100ml boiling water
100g smoked salmon
black onion seeds, to sprinkle
radishes or Crudités (see
  opposite)

PREPARATION TIME
10 minutes

COOKING TIME
10 minutes

WALNUT BAGNA CAUDA

This is a recipe for which I have been searching for years. I first tried it at the famous London Italian restaurant San Lorenzo, and it has stuck with me forever. Traditionally bagna cauda is made as an oil- and butter-based dipping sauce, but my mum and I remember it being very walnutty. I researched the recipe and couldn't find a version with walnuts in it anywhere, but I did find some versions using walnut oil. I've totally made up this version, but it's pretty damn close to the original and, more importantly, it's delicious.

Heat the olive oil in a saucepan, then add the garlic and fry it very slowly in the oil for about 1–2 minutes, or until the garlic has tinged a little golden. Add the anchovies and let them melt away into the oil. Next, add the walnuts and gently toast them for 1 minute. Add the double cream and butter and cook for 2 minutes, or until the mixture is piping hot, and then finish with the walnut oil and lemon juice.

Now you need to blend this to a purée in a small blender. You want it to be the texture of a thin, creamy hummus, almost like a thick, coating-consistency salad dressing. Transfer the bagna cauda to a heatproof pot with a flame underneath (the obvious choice would be a fondue pot) and plunge away at it with your Crudités.

150ml extra virgin olive oil
3–4 garlic cloves, finely
  chopped
8 anchovies
100g walnuts
150ml double cream
30g butter
30ml walnut oil
1 teaspoon lemon juice
Crudités (see page 36)

PICKLED VEGETABLE PATCH SALAD

Angela Hartnett and Luke Holder have a restaurant at Lime Wood hotel called Hartnett Holder & Co. They grow everything on site and even make their own charcuterie. One of the dishes they do is a BRILLIANT sharing platter that looks just like a vegetable patch, and this is my version of that dish, complete with a cheat's olive soil. The pickled veg are just awesome on their own but this whole salad platter makes a really cool starter or part of a buffet (which, by the way, I'm all about bringing back...).

Melt the vinegar, sugar, salt, thyme and chilli in a saucepan, and then pour over the vegetables in a large non-reactive bowl. Cover with cling film and leave until cool – this will take about 2 hours.

To make the olive soil, place the olives in a food processor and blitz. The blitzed olives will be quite wet so lay them on some kitchen paper and squeeze out the excess liquid. Transfer to a bowl.

Next, blend half the seeds with the salt in a food processor until they're dust. Transfer to a bowl, add the remaining seeds and mix well.

To serve, mash up and spread the goat's curd in a line on the base of a large platter, then spread a line of the the olive soil and finally a line of seeds. Arrange the vegetables in rows on top to make it slightly resemble a vegetable garden. Drizzle with the oil, bring to the table and scoff straightaway, either by scooping up and plating or just dipping into the elements.

100g pitted black olives

100g toasted mixed seeds, sesame, sunflower and pumpkin seeds are best)

½ teaspoon salt

300g goat's curd

2 tablespoons rapeseed or really good extra virgin olive oil

For the vegetables

500ml white wine or cider vinegar

200g golden caster sugar

60g fine salt

1 thyme sprig

1 small dried chilli or a pinch of dried chilli flakes

60g cauliflower, cut into florets

60g romanesco cauliflower, cut into florets

60g purple cauliflower, cut into florets

a small bunch of baby carrots, trimmed and tidied

2 baby fennel bulbs, cut in half lengthways

12 radishes with leaves

SERVES 4
....

PREPARATION TIME
30 minutes, plus cooling

COOKING TIME
20 minutes

BHEL PURI SALAD WITH HEIRLOOM TOMATOES

Indian food is just wonderful and so diverse. I was introduced to bhel puri by Horn OK Please, an Indian street-food company. Bhel puri is basically a salad of vegetables and onions mixed with crunchy puffed rice and chickpea noodles (both of which can be bought from Indian supermarkets), a date and tamarind chutney and a green chutney. It's sweet, sour, spicy, crunchy, fresh and such a healthy snack. I've used great British heirloom tomatoes and chickpeas in this recipe and made the dish into a bit more of a salad. If you have any of the chutney left over, serve it with puris or poppadums or alongside curries: for me, it beats mango chutney and raita every time.

....

For the date & tamarind chutney

14 dates, pitted
1 tablespoon dried tamarind, rehydrated in 250ml boiling water
1 tablespoon jaggery, palm sugar or brown sugar
1 teaspoon chat or garam masala
1 teaspoon ground cumin
½ teaspoon red chilli powder

For the green chutney dressing

1 small packet (about 30g) of coriander, leaves picked
a handful of mint leaves
2 green chillies, deseeded if you don't want the dressing to be too spicy
3cm piece of fresh root ginger, peeled
1 teaspoon cumin seeds, toasted
¼ teaspoon garam masala
3 tablespoons lemon juice
a good pinch of salt

For the salad

700g heirloom tomatoes (a mixture of different colours, varieties and sizes)
¼ teaspoon fine salt or enough to season your tomatoes
1 red onion, finely chopped
1 cucumber, peeled and finely diced
seeds from 1 pomegranate
1 x 400g can chickpeas, drained
a bunch of coriander, roughly chopped
30g Indian puffed rice (this looks like long Rice Krispies)
60g plain bhujia (chickpea noodles)

To make the date and tamarind chutney, place all the ingredients in a blender and blitz together until smooth. It will be a fairly thin chutney but you don't want any lumps in it, so make sure you blend it until it is really smooth. Pour into a saucepan and cook down slowly over a lowish heat for 20 minutes, or until the flavours are rich, homogenized and cooked out and the chutney has thickened to the consistency of a thick ketchup. Set aside to cool.

To make the green chutney dressing, place all the ingredients in a small blender and blitz until a smooth paste. Set aside.

Now you need to get on with making your salad. Cut the tomatoes into a variety of different shapes and sizes and place in a bowl with the salt. Add all the remaining salad ingredients except for the puffed rice and bhujia. Pour over the date and tamarind chutney and the green chutney dressing and mix thoroughly. Next, add two-thirds of the puffed rice and bhujia and mix quickly – the salad will make popping noises, just like when you add milk to Rice Krispies.

To serve, divide the salad between 4 plates, and then sprinkle over the remaining puffed rice and bhujia. Eat straightaway so that the crispy ingredients don't get soggy!

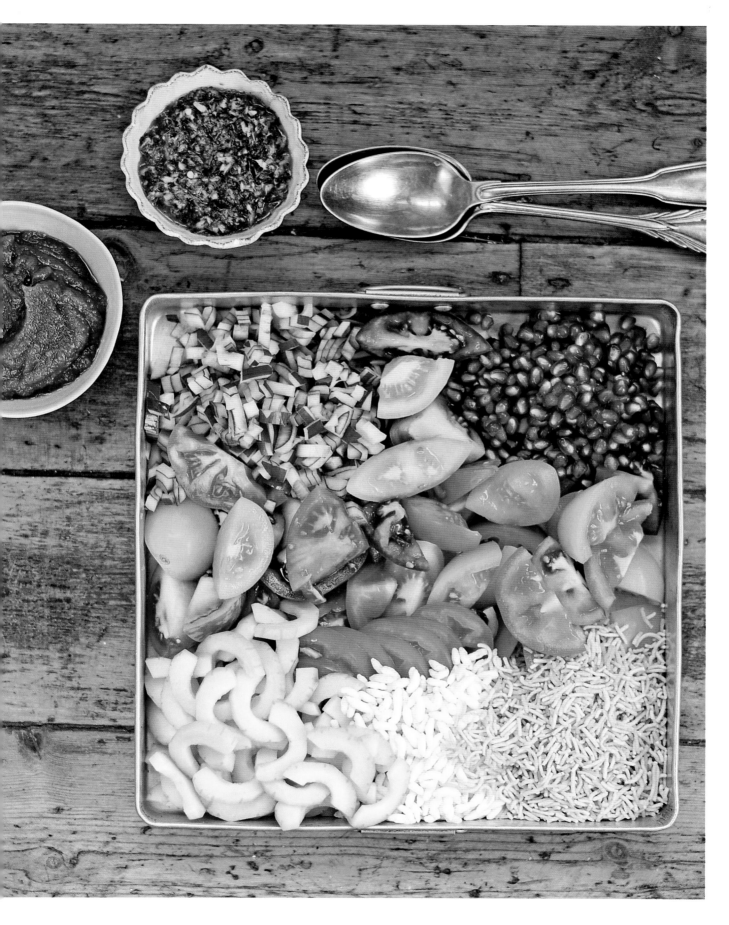

AVOCADO SALAD WITH WASABI, WAKAME & SPRING ONIONS

Avocado is not a traditional Japanese ingredient, though we do associate it with Japanese cuisine due to the brilliant Japanese fusion food that comes out of California. Avocado just works so well with Japanese flavours. This salad also includes wasabi, which is Japanese horseradish, for those of you still living in the Dark Ages, and wakame, which is dried and then rehydrated seaweed. This healthy salad is delicious on its own and is also great served alongside teriyaki or miso fish.

Place the wakame in a heatproof bowl and cover with boiling water. Leave to soak for 15 minutes. The wakame will rehydrate and grow in size, so cover with plenty of water to allow for this. It's ready when it has doubled in size and you can bite through it but it still has chew. Drain, and then rinse under cold running water to cool. Alternatively, you can cool the wakame in a bowl of iced water. Drain again and gently pat dry with kitchen paper.

To make the dressing, place the wasabi, vinegar, oils and some seasoning in a bowl and whisk together until it has fully emulsified into a thickish sauce.

Cut the avocados in half, remove the stones and then peel off the skins. Slice the halved avocados and place on a platter. Once you've done this, gently press the top of the avocados to fan out the slices a little. Top with the dressing, then the wakame, then the radishes, then the spring onions and finally sprinkle over the sesame seeds. Serve straightaway.

25g dried wakame seaweed
4 ripe but firm avocados
10 pink radishes, very thinly sliced
6 spring onions, finely chopped
1 tablespoon black sesame seeds, toasted
1 tablespoon white sesame seeds, toasted

For the dressing

3 teaspoons wasabi paste (use the best you can find)
4 tablespoons rice wine vinegar
4 tablespoons light olive oil
2 tablespoons sesame oil
sea salt flakes and freshly ground black pepper

CEVICHE WITH YUZU, SESAME & KUMQUATS

1 large wild sea bass, about
   800g–1kg, filleted and
   skinned
1 corn on the cob, husk removed
olive oil
1 large ripe avocado, peeled,
   stoned and cut into small
   cubes
6 kumquats, thinly sliced
   horizontally into 6 or 7
   pieces and pipped
½ large red onion, very thinly
   sliced
a few coriander leaves, roughly
   chopped

For the 'tigers milk'

1 garlic clove, finely grated
1 large hot red chilli or 2
   small ones, deseeded and
   finely chopped
¾ teaspoon salt
60ml yuzu juice
2 tablespoons soy sauce
2 tablespoons sesame oil

The first time that I had ceviche was when I was 21 years old and on a beach in Tulum, Mexico. When I was younger I was a bit freaked about eating sushi and the idea of eating raw fish that had been macerated in lime juice (which is essentially what ceviche is) made me feel much the same. I can't tell you how it works exactly but the citrus juice cooks the fish and I mean COOKS it. If you leave your ceviche to macerate for long enough the fish will be cooked all the way through. In fact, you're curing the fish at the same time as you're marinating it. This process also gives the fish tons of flavour. A lot of Latin American coastal countries claim ceviche as their own. It's a classic Peruvian dish and if there is one thing I know about Peruvian cuisine it's that it is a mishmash of many cultures: genuine fusion food. Martin Morales, from the restaurant Ceviche, once told me that there are no rules in Peruvian cooking and this gives him free rein to play with his food. Martin has used passion fruit and pomegranate in his ceviche; both are acidic fruits with a different tang that work brilliantly with the fish. I love Japanese fusion food, so here I've combined yuzu and sesame (the flavours from my favourite sashimi dish) with kumquats, the tiny citrus fruits that have an acidic flesh and super-sweet skins. And what do you know? It's a triumph!

···

Cut the fish into thick slices of sashimi, about 4mm thick. Put the fish in a mixing bowl, cover with cling film and place in the fridge. I do this first as it's good to have all the ingredients ready to go when the time comes to construct the dish.

Next, heat a griddle pan until it's smoking. Rub the corn with some oil, and then griddle it on all sides until it's charred all over but the corn is still firm. Remove from the heat and leave to cool for 5 minutes. Then, using a sharp knife, carve off the corn kernels and place them in a bowl with the avocado and kumquats.

To make the 'tigers milk', pound together the garlic, chilli and salt in a mortar with a pestle, slowly trickling in the yuzu juice, soy sauce and sesame oil. 'Tigers milk' is the sauce that's used to dress the ceviche. When you mix the sauce with the fish it goes a little milky from the protein.

Once you're ready to rock-and-roll, add the red onion and the 'tigers milk' to a non-reactive bowl, add the fish and give it a good stir. Pop it back in the fridge and leave for 5 minutes. I like my fish to still be a little raw in the middle but if you prefer your fish to be more 'cooked' then you can leave it in the fridge for up to 20 minutes. Next, add the sweetcorn, avocado, kumquats and coriander to the bowl and give it another good stir to combine. Leave for a further 5 minutes, then stir again and serve straightaway. Some people serve ceviche in glasses or alongside a small fried corn tortilla or with tortilla chips, so feel free to go to town if you want to.

PREPARATION TIME
30 minutes, plus drying
overnight

COOKING TIME
1½ hours

THAI ROAST DUCK & WATERMELON SALAD

One of my most memorable cooking experiences was when I worked at Min Jiang at the Royal Garden Hotel in Kensington, which is famous for its roast duck and dim sum. I spent a day learning all the secrets to the perfect Crispy Peking Duck. It's no mean feat. First, air is blown under the duck's skin to separate the skin from the flesh. The duck is doused in searing hot syrup to constrict and glaze the skin, then it is left to dry overnight. It's then roasted at a really hot temperature and actually served pink. The skin is carved away and the duck is sliced rather than shredded and served with plum sauce, spring onions, cucumber and pancakes. I've made my recipe a bit more user-friendly. Essentially, you are just giving the duck a hot bath in molten liquor for a few minutes before drying it out in the fridge overnight and then roasting it. It's no more effort than marinating something the night before, just a little more unusual. I've paired the duck with the most deelish Thai watermelon salad, inspired by chef Ian Pengelley, but feel free to serve the duck the classic way with pancakes if you prefer.

....

2 litres water
1 star anise
1 slice of galangal or ginger, bruised
2 spring onions, split down the middle
5 tablespoons maltose or (if you really can't find it) honey
4 tablespoons light soy sauce
2 tablespoons salt
1 free-range duck, about 1.2–3kg, not too fatty
Thai Salad Dressing (see opposite)
lime wedges, to serve

For the salad

½ medium watermelon, cut into small cubes
100g cashew nuts or peanuts, roasted
a small handful of Thai basil leaves
a small handful of mint leaves
a small handful of coriander leaves
1 shallot, finely sliced
Crispy Shallots (see page 79)

You will also need a saucepan large enough to fit the whole duck

Place the water, star anise, galangal or ginger, spring onions, maltose or honey, soy sauce and salt in the saucepan and bring to the boil. Turn off the heat and leave to infuse for 10 minutes. Bring back to the boil, scoop out the aromatics, and then plunge the duck, skin-side up, into the water and immerse it fully. You may need to keep it pushed down with a wooden spoon. Bring to the boil for 3 minutes, then quickly remove the duck and dry fully on kitchen paper.

Clear a shelf in the fridge, lay a few sheets of cling film on the shelf, and then place some kitchen paper on top. Next, lay a wire rack on top of this. Place the duck on the wire rack and leave to dry in the fridge for 15 hours. The duck skin will feel like wax paper when it's dry.

Preheat the oven to 200°C/Gas Mark 6. Place the duck on a rack in an oven tray and fill the tray with 300ml water. If you want classic roast Chinese duck that's still pink, roast the duck for 40 minutes, or until the skin is crisp and golden;

if you want crispy duck, cook for 60 minutes, turning the oven down to 180°C/Gas Mark 4 after 30 minutes. Leave the duck to rest for 10 minutes before carving. Carve off the legs and use two forks to shred the leg meat, removing the bones as you go. Next, if you're serving your duck pink, remove the breasts with the skin intact and cut widthways into slices; or you can shred it like crispy duck. Sprinkle over a tiny bit of salt, then arrange on one side of a large serving platter.

Place the watermelon on the platter and scatter over the nuts, herbs, shallot slices and Crispy Shallots. Serve with the Thai Salad Dressing and lime wedges.

THAI SALAD DRESSING

SERVES 4

150ml water
200g palm sugar
3-4 Thai red chillies, sliced
1 lemon grass stick, bruised
1 small piece of galangal or
  fresh root ginger, about
  5cm x 2.5cm, bruised
5 lime leaves, torn
2 tablespoons tamarind paste
2 tablespoons fish sauce
2 tablespoons lime juice

Boil all the ingredients together in a saucepan over a medium heat for about 5 minutes, or until it has reduced and is like honey. It needs to be thicker and more potent than your average dressing because it will be diluted with all the juice the watermelon lets out. Leave to cool.

SERVES 4
....

PREPARATION TIME
20 minutes

COOKING TIME
15 minutes

SUPERFOOD SALAD

This salad has everything you could possibly want for health: oily fish for brain development and building a good heart, and a variety of green vegetables for balancing alkalinity in the blood. Kale is a winner in salads but you need to give it a really quick blanch first or it's like eating tickly autumn leaves. The avocado is full of vitamin E and good oils that will help you burn fat, and it's the same deal with the seeds. There's quinoa for carbs and more protein and we're toasting it to give it a more nutty flavour. The Japanese dressing with shallots and ginger will cleanse your blood and give it some spunk.

....

Pop the quinoa in a dry frying pan and toast over a medium heat, keeping the quinoa moving the whole time, until it's lightly golden and nutty. Transfer to a small saucepan and add a good pinch of salt and the water. Cover, bring to the boil and cook for 10 minutes. Remove from the heat and, keeping the lid on, let the quinoa steam for 5 minutes to soak up the remaining liquid and get fluffy.

To make the dressing, place all the ingredients in a clean jam jar and season with salt and pepper. Screw the lid on tightly and shake it like crazy.

Drain the kale and dry it on kitchen paper, then roughly chop. Place the kale in a large salad bowl along with the edamame beans, broccoli, avocado, spring onions, radishes and quinoa. Dress with two-thirds of the salad dressing, give a swift mix so as not to let the avocado break up too much, then plate up between 4 plates. Top with the salmon and the remaining dressing and finish with a scattering of the sesame seeds.

100g quinoa
320ml water
100g kale, blanched for
  30 seconds and refreshed
  in iced water
100g fresh or frozen edamame
  beans
½ head of broccoli, cut into
  small florets
1 avocado, peeled, stoned and
  chopped
2 spring onions, thinly sliced
10 radishes, thinly sliced
300g perfectly cooked or
  hot-smoked salmon, skin
  removed and flesh flaked
1 tablespoon toasted black and/
  or white sesame seeds

For the Japanese salad dressing

1 banana shallot, very finely
  chopped
3cm piece of fresh root ginger,
  peeled and grated
6 tablespoons rice wine vinegar
6 tablespoons soy sauce
6 tablespoons sesame oil
sea salt flakes and freshly
  ground black pepper

....

GRIDDLED MARINATED WHOLE CHICKEN CAESAR SALAD

I'm not really a salad kinda gal. I like food that's a bit more buxom. I need to have a major protein hit if I'm going to really enjoy my food, and the balance in most salads isn't quite right. Chicken salads piss me off. Mostly because they are made with chicken breasts and I prefer my meat on the bone but also because they're built to be quite delicate. I'm 5ft 10in and a broad-shouldered tomboy, certainly not delicate. The flavours of Caesar salad fit my brief: Parmesan, anchovy and garlic all smack you round the chops. It's a good salad. But it's a better salad when served alongside a whole griddled chicken.

1 medium free-range chicken, spatchcocked
1 bulb of garlic, cloves peeled and finely chopped
3 tablespoons chopped herbs (I would go for thyme, rosemary and parsley)
2 tablespoons Korean or regular chilli powder
1 teaspoon sea salt flakes
freshly ground black pepper
grated rind and juice of 1 lemon
2 tablespoons olive oil

For the croutons

100ml olive oil
4 garlic cloves, bashed
2 rosemary sprigs
¼ white loaf or white sourdough bread, trimmed of crusts and torn into bite-sized pieces

For the salad

2 Romaine lettuces or 4 Little Gem lettuces, sliced
Light Caesar Dressing (see opposite)
4 free-range eggs (I like to use Cotswold Legbar or Burford Brown eggs), soft-boiled for 6 minutes
8 pickled anchovies, sliced in half lengthways
30g Parmesan cheese, shaved

Lay the spatchcocked chicken in a roasting tray. Using a pestle and mortar, bash together the garlic, herbs, chilli, salt and pepper and lemon rind, gradually adding the lemon juice and oil. Rub this marinade all over the chicken, cover with cling film and leave in the fridge overnight to marinate.

To make the croutons, preheat the oven to 180°C/Gas Mark 4. Place the oil, garlic and rosemary in a saucepan and heat until the garlic and herbs start to sizzle. Remove from the heat and leave to stand for 10 minutes. Strain the garlic and herbs from the oil and set both the infused oil and the garlic and herbs aside. Lay the bread in a roasting tray and drizzle with the infused oil. Roast for 25 minutes, turning the croutons halfway through, until golden on the outside. I don't like dried out croutons; I prefer them to have a bit of give in the middle.

Heat a griddle pan until smoking and cook the chicken on each side until lightly charred. Return the chicken to the roasting tray and cook in the oven for 25 minutes, or until the juices in the legs run clear. Chop the chicken through its joints into 10 pieces.

Pop the lettuce leaves into a bowl and dress with half the dressing. Place the leaves on a platter and pour the other half of the dressing over the leaves. Cut the boiled eggs in half and place on top along with the anchovies, Parmesan shavings and reserved crispy rosemary sprigs and croutons. Serve alongside the griddled chicken with the chicken juices poured over.

LIGHT CAESAR DRESSING

My girly addition to this recipe is the salad dressing, which I've made much lighter by using less oil and replacing some of the oil with natural yogurt. The tang of the yogurt is great with the vinegar and it cuts down the calories. So I might be a tomboy but my butt likes me to remember to keep myself in check!

SERVES 4-6

1 egg yolk
5 anchovies in oil
1 teaspoon Dijon mustard
1 tablespoon white wine
  vinegar
50g Parmesan cheese, grated
2 garlic cloves (you can use
  the cooked leftover garlic
  from making the croutons
  opposite)
200ml light olive oil
100g natural yogurt
juice of 1 lemon
sea salt flakes and freshly
  ground black pepper

Put the egg yolk, anchovies, mustard, vinegar, Parmesan and garlic cloves in a food processor and blend until smooth. Continue to blend and slowly trickle in the oil until the dressing thickens up. Mix in the yogurt and season with the lemon juice and salt and pepper.

PREPARATION TIME
25 minutes, plus 2 hours
salting

COOKING TIME
40 minutes

SOFIA'S PINKALILLI

I have a sidekick who helps me with everything. Her name is Sofia. I couldn't do what I do without her. She is a beautiful girl in her mid-twenties from Sweden, but don't let her looks fool you — this girl is a powerhouse. I dread the day she wants to leave me. I asked her to contribute a recipe to the book, and knowing me so well she went with a classic recipe but made it hot pink. So here we have Sofia's pinkalilli recipe. It's based on a classic piccalilli but made with beetroot. Serve it with a pork pie, sausage rolls, cured meats — basically anything porky.

200g beetroot, peeled and cut
  into bite-sized pieces
  (keeping the peel)
600ml white wine vinegar
150g runner beans, cut into 1cm
  bite-sized pieces
150g French beans, each trimmed
  and cut into 4 pieces
½ large cauliflower, cut into
  small florets
2 courgettes, cut into 1cm or
  bite-sized pieces
200g silverskin onions, frozen
  and then defrosted
35g fine salt
3 baby cucumbers, deseeded and
  cut into 1cm or bite-sized
  pieces
1 bay leaf
1½ teaspoons mustard seeds
2 garlic cloves, crushed
3cm piece of fresh root ginger,
  peeled and grated
150g golden caster sugar
1 tablespoon English mustard
  powder
1 tablespoon plain flour
1 teaspoon cornflour

Put the beetroot peel and vinegar in a non-reactive bowl and set aside.

Lay the runner beans, French beans, cauliflower, courgettes and onions in a colander and sprinkle with most of the salt, reserving ½ tablespoon of salt for the cucumber, and set aside for 2 hours. For the final 30 minutes, lay the cucumber in a separate colander and sprinkle with the reserved salt.

Rinse the vegetables well and drain. Put the runner beans, French beans, cauliflower, courgettes, onions and beetroot in a large casserole dish.

Remove the beetroot peel from the vinegar and discard. Add the vinegar to the casserole together with the bay leaf, mustard seeds, garlic and ginger. Bring to a simmer and cook gently until the vegetables are just beginning to soften but still have a bite to them. Add the cucumber and sugar and cook for 3–4 minutes. Set a large colander over a bowl, strain the vegetables, and then pour the vinegar liquor into a measuring jug.

In a large saucepan, mix together the mustard powder, plain flour and cornflour, add about 3 tablespoons of the vinegar liquor and whisk until smooth, then stir in the rest of the liquor. Set the pan over a medium heat and cook, stirring all the time, until the sauce starts to thicken. Cook gently for about 8–10 minutes, or until the sauce has the consistency of thick cream. Add the vegetables to the sauce and mix well.

Transfer to 4–6 sterilized jars and seal tightly. Keep in the fridge for up to a year, or use within 1 month of opening.

MAKES 100g

....

PREPARATION TIME
5 minutes

COOKING TIME
5 minutes

TOASTED BLACK SESAME BUTTER

Black sesame butter sounds like a revelation but has been used in Asian cooking for years. It's the base of a lot of Korean and Japanese dishes, and I've been using it for everything from ice cream to Korean rice porridge. I started making my own when I became obsessed with making different-flavoured nut butters. I tested them on apples and bits of crackers, and I started to get a taste for this one as a kind of butter rather than the simple sesame paste it was known for. I added a spot of sweetness and some salt. Now it's fully addictive straight from the jar and eaten in the same way as you would peanut butter, but also in dressings and as a tahini in dips. It may look like tar and taste like its utterly filthy for you, but those little black sesame seeds are high in protein, packed with virtually every mineral going and great for reducing cholesterol. It tastes bloody lovely to boot.

....

Place the sesame seeds in a dry pan and toast them over a low heat for about 5 minutes. It's hard to tell with black sesame seeds when they are toasted but you need to judge with your nose. Its important they are well toasted otherwise the butter will taste a little bitter and raw, but be careful not to burn them.

Place these in a high-power food processor and blitz until the seeds have broken up. Next add in the oil, maple and salt and blitz for at least 30 seconds, or until fully blended. Transfer into a sterilized jam jar and seal firmly. This will last for weeks if you can avoid guzzling it all.

100g black sesame seeds
4-5 tablespoons sesame oil
   (NOT TOASTED) or vegetable oil
1 tablespoon maple syrup
a good pinch of sea salt flakes

....

CRISP

FRIED & CRUMBED

PREPARATION TIME
20 minutes, plus chilling
overnight

COOKING TIME
10 minutes

CHOPPED LIVER WITH EGG & GRIBENES

Chopped liver is like a coarse **pâté**. Traditionally, it's made by frying chicken livers with onions, hand-chopping and then mixing with schmaltz. I have taken some French **pâté**-making techniques and used them to make **pâté**'s Jewish brother, slowly cooking shallots with port and Madeira to add sweetness and body to complement the livers before blitzing them in a blender to a still-rough but slightly smoother texture.

350g chicken livers
150ml Schmaltz (see page 216)
3 large shallots, finely
 chopped
a few thyme sprigs
2 tablespoons Madeira
2 tablespoons port
generous grating of nutmeg
sea salt flakes and freshly
 ground black pepper

To serve

2 hard-boiled free-range eggs
 (I love Cotswold Legbar eggs
 as they have orange yolks),
 grated
100g Gribenes (see page 216)
1 tablespoon finely chopped
 parsley
a few dill sprigs
toasted challah or matzoh
 crackers
dill pickles and/or new green
 pickles, sliced

Prepare the chicken livers by removing the vascular centres carefully with a knife. Season with plenty of salt and pepper.

Heat 2 tablespoons of schmaltz in a frying pan. When hot, add the chicken livers and fry until brown on all sides. You need to make sure that the livers are cooked through but still very pink in the middles or the finished dish will be grey rather than the parfait pink that you want it to be. Set the livers aside on a plate.

Wipe the pan clean with kitchen paper to remove any scorched bits, then add 3 more tablespoons of schmaltz to the pan. Add the shallots and thyme and fry over a lower heat for about 5 minutes, or until they have softened enough that you can squash them with your fingertips. Pour over the Madeira and port, bring to the boil and cook for 1–2 minutes, or until the liquid has disappeared and the shallots are bright pink. Remove the thyme and set aside to cool for 10 minutes.

Put the livers, shallots, the remaining schmaltz, nutmeg and some salt and pepper in a food processor. Blitz on the pulse mode until the mixture forms a rough pâté-like paste. Transfer to a terrine or plastic container and top with greaseproof paper to stop the surface oxidizing. Wrap the terrine or container tightly with cling film and refrigerate overnight.

Remove the pâté from the fridge 10 minutes before serving. Unwrap the terrine or container and heat 2 serving spoons in boiling water. Dry the spoons and use them to make a quenelle of pâté to place on each plate. Sprinkle some grated egg, Gribenes and herbs over the top of each quenelle and serve with matzoh crackers or toasted challah and some pickles.

SERVES 9
....

PREPARATION TIME
20 minutes

COOKING TIME
40 minutes

POTATO LATKES

Latkes remind me of going to NYC with my manager, who is like my big sister, and eating the hugest salt-beef sandwiches, bowls of chicken noodle soup, chopped liver, egg and onions, and latkes with soured cream. I ended up smearing the latkes with everything served at the dinner table. I love latkes — they are like rösti but better. I love them served with cream cheese and smoked salmon for breakfast, or with fried eggs, or with... basically anything!

Heat the butter in frying pan over a medium heat and fry the onion for 10 minutes, or until softened. Set aside.

Grate the potatoes on the coarse holes of a grater, then transfer the grated potatoes to a large colander set over a large bowl. Squeeze the water out of the potatoes, letting the liquid drip through the holes of the colander into the bowl. Let this liquid sit in the bowl for few minutes, then carefully pour out the water but keep the layer of pale beige paste at the bottom of the bowl. This is potato starch, which will help your latkes stick together.

Add the potatoes, onion, egg yolks, matzoh meal and salt to the potato starch and give it all a good mix until everything is evenly incorporated.

Preheat the oven to 180°C/Gas Mark 4.

In a separate, spotlessly clean bowl, whisk the egg whites until stiff, then fold them into the potato mixture.

Heat 2 tablespoons of oil in a frying pan and spoon a couple of tablespoons of the potato mixture into the pan and fry for few minutes on each side, or until the latkes are nice and golden. Repeat until you have used up all the mixture. Transfer the finished latkes to a baking tray and bake for 15 minutes, or until they are all cooked through. Serve with soured cream or cream cheese and apple sauce and season with black pepper.

1 tablespoon butter
1 large onion, finely chopped
6 large Maris Piper potatoes, scrubbed
2 free-range eggs, separated
2 tablespoons matzoh meal
2 teaspoons salt
corn or vegetable oil, for frying

To serve
soured cream or cream cheese
apple sauce
freshly ground black pepper

NACHOS WITH REFRIED BEANS

My best night in ever is watching a good horror movie and having my fill of chips and dips. And the best way to have chips and dips is with nachos. I prefer my nachos with refried beans instead of chilli con carne – and it's not often you'll see me choose veggie over meat. Making your own refried beans is easy and so much tastier than the shop-bought options. I've used pinto beans as they are classic, but the recipe works well with red kidney and black beans too.

150g plain tortilla chips
100g Cheddar cheese, grated
Guacamole (see opposite)
80g soured cream
3 tablespoons sliced pickled
  jalepeños
coriander leaves, to garnish

For the salsa

3–4 tomatoes, deseeded and
  finely chopped
1 red chilli, deseeded and
  finely chopped
1 garlic clove, grated
juice of 1 large juicy lime
½ teaspoon sea salt flakes
½ tablespoon extra virgin olive
  oil

For the refried beans

4 tablespoons lard or (even
  better) bacon fat or use any
  cooking oil you like
1 onion, finely chopped
6 garlic cloves, finely chopped
1 tablespoon cumin seeds
1 teaspoon ground coriander
1 x 400g can pinto beans,
  drained and washed
300ml fresh White Chicken or
  Veggie Stock (see pages
  212–13)
sea salt flakes and freshly
  ground black pepper

Make the salsa by mixing together the tomatoes, chilli, garlic, lime juice, salt and olive oil in a bowl. Set aside to macerate while you make the rest of the dish. By the time you get to use the salsa it will be really watery: that's the salt taking the water out of the tomatoes. Drain off this water but don't throw it away or I will hunt you down! Drink it – it's pure essence of tomato and the yummiest thing on the planet.

To make the refried beans, heat the lard, fat or oil in a frying pan. Add the onion and fry slowly for about 10 minutes, or until soft and lightly golden, adding the garlic and cumin seeds during the final 1–2 minutes. Add the ground coriander and fry for a further 30 seconds. Add the beans, stir to coat with the oniony spices, and then pour over the stock. Bring to a gentle boil, then reduce the heat and cook over a low heat for 10 minutes. When there are only about 3 tablespoons of the liquid left, blend the beans in a food processor until smooth. Wipe the frying pan clean and then return the beans to the pan (you may need a spot more lard, fat or oil when doing this, depending on how nonstick your pan is). Fry the beans for about 5 minutes or until they change colour and thicken up (they should be like a thick hummus). Season to taste with plenty of salt and pepper.

Preheat the oven to 200°C/Gas Mark 6.

Place the tortilla chips in an ovenproof bowl and top with the cheese. Bake them for 10 minutes, or until the cheese has melted. Remove from the oven and top with a layer of the hot refried beans – it looks like loads but I swear you need it all. Next, top this with a good 2 tablespoons of guacamole, then the same amount of salsa and the same amount of soured cream. Sprinkle over the jalepeños, garnish with coriander and you're good to go!

GUACAMOLE

SERVES 2-4

2 very ripe avocados, skins and stones removed
juice of 1 large lime
1 chilli, deseeded (unless you like it spicy) and finely chopped
1 garlic clove, grated
pinch of ground cumin
1 large ripe tomato, deseeded and finely chopped
2 spring onions, finely sliced
sea salt flakes and freshly ground black pepper

To make the guacamole, mash the avocado in a mortar with a pestle or in a bowl with a fork. Mix in the lime juice, chilli, garlic, ground cumin, tomato and spring onions and season with salt and pepper. Lay some cling film over the top of the guacamole and set aside.

KOREAN FRIED CHICKEN

200ml buttermilk
1 tablespoon salt
8 free-range or organic chicken
  wings, wing tips cut off,
  then each wing cut in half
  through the joint to make
  16 pieces
oil, for deep-frying
2 tablespoons toasted sesame
  seeds (white, black or a
  mixture of both)
2 spring onions, (green parts
  only), very thinly sliced
  into rings, to garnish

For the sauce

2 tablespoons gochujang (Korean
  chilli paste)
2 tablespoons Sriracha chilli
  sauce
4 tablespoons caster suger
4 tablespoons rice wine vinegar
2 tablespoons ketchup
1 tablespoon sesame oil
1 tablespoon chicken fat or
  butter

For the flour mix

6 tablespoons self-raising
  flour
3 tablespoons rice flour
3 tablespoons potato flour
sea salt flakes and white
  pepper

This is a recipe that I have made a thousand times and developed over the past six years, having first tried them in K-town in New York at the advice of my friend, chef Judy Joo. It's now (I guess) my 'signature dish' and it makes an appearance at pretty much every event, take-over or pop-up that I do, though I've never fully published it until now. I am writing this recipe while in Seoul and for the first time I feel that I can finally put it to bed after having eaten mountains of Korean fried chicken from its motherland and knowing for sure that I now have it right. My recipe is a fusion of American meets Asian, brining the wings first to tenderize, season and firm up the wings then tossing them in three flours. You might think this step is a bit extreme but each flour does its own thing: the self-raising (wheat) flour is for puff, the potato flour is for chew and the rice flour gives it crunch. Don't mess about with this step. The wings are then fried over a low heat until cooked, dried and then flash-fried on high, making them crisp and drawing out the juices to form an umami crust. Finally, they are tossed in an addictive Korean chilli sauce to coat the wings, then in sesame seeds and garnished with very finely sliced spring onions. Serve them the Korean way, piled into mountains alongside a stack of imported beer while watching football or K-pop with pals.

··

Mix the buttermilk and salt together in a bowl. Add the chicken wings and massage the brine into the wings, then leave in the fridge for 12–24 hours. This will draw out all the excess water from the wings, leaving the concentrated chicken juices.

To make the sauce, melt together the gochujang, chilli sauce, sugar, vinegar, ketchup, sesame oil and chicken fat or butter in a saucepan. Bring to the boil for a minute, then remove from the heat and set aside.

Mix all the flours together in a bowl and season well. Take the wings out of the buttermilk brine, wiping off any excess with kitchen paper. Toss the wings, 4 pieces at a time, in the flours. Remove and set aside.

Heat the oil in a deep-fat fryer (or a deep saucepan or wok filled with oil a third of the way up its sides) to 140°C. Add the wings and fry gently (or confit) for 8–10 minutes, or until they are cooked through but have barely taken on any colour. Remove the wings and drain on kitchen paper. Increase the temperature of the oil to 190°C and fry the wings for a further 2–3 minutes, or until they are golden and cooked through.

Toss the wings in the sauce and 1 tablespoon of the sesame seeds. Sprinkle over the remaining sesame seeds and the spring onions and serve immediately. These are best eaten with your fingers and served with an ice-cold beer.

WET & WILD GARLIC CHICKEN KIEVS

Chicken Kievs are utterly delicious — I am squealing inside while I write this recipe and wait for them to cook. Garlic butter makes everything taste good and so does frying anything in breadcrumbs, so here we have a double whammy of deliciousness. Chicken Kievs are a little complicated to make (they must be sealed well, the butter needs to be frozen and you have to make sure you slit the chicken evenly so that the butter can't seep out) but it's a fun process and a good one to get your hands dirty with. I've pimped up my recipe by roasting fresh wild garlic and then adding this, plus some grated garlic AND some wild garlic, to the butter and then wrapping it in wild garlic leaves. And these chicken Kievs are — I can say this because I've just tasted them — possibly the best thing I've ever eaten. You can quote me on that.

···

16 wild garlic leaves
Garlic Butter (see opposite)
2 large free-range eggs, beaten
  with a little milk
100g plain flour, seasoned with
  salt and pepper
300g panko breadcrumbs
4 large free-range chicken
  breasts with fillets attached
  (I like using supremes, which
  you can get from your
  butcher, as they still have
  the wing tip attached)
oil, for deep-frying

Take the whole wild garlic leaves and lay them out on a work surface, 4 leaves per chicken breast. Divide the butter between the 4 sets of leaves and roll them up to make 4 parcels about the size and shape of your thumb. Wrap the parcels in cling film and then place them in the freezer for 20–30 minutes, or until they are very firm. (If I have any excess butter, I melt it and serve it poured over the cooked chicken Kievs).

When the butter is hard, take 3 bowls and fill one with the seasoned flour, one with the beaten eggs and one with the breadcrumbs. Using a sharp knife, make a deep cut lengthways along each chicken breast to make a pocket in the chicken. Stick your finger in the pocket and root around a bit to make the hole a little bit larger. Unwrap the cling film from the frozen butter parcels and stuff each breast with one of the parcels. Plug up the hole in each chicken breast with the false fillet, or a bit of the false fillet, and pinch the end of the chicken shut.

Lower the oven temperature to 190°C/Gas Mark 5. Heat the oil in either a deep-fat fryer or a deep saucepan to 190°C. Carefully dip each stuffed breast first in the seasoned flour, then in plenty of the egg, and then in the breadcrumbs, coating them thoroughly and paying particular attention to the end where they've been sealed. I would double-coat the end with more egg and breadcrumbs.

Carefully place each chicken Kiev into the hot oil and cook for 4–5 minutes, or until the Kievs turn a light golden colour. Transfer to a baking tray and bake for 12–15 minutes, until cooked through and nicely crisp and brown. Some of the butter will have leaked out, so be sure to pour that back over the chicken when you serve it. Serve the chicken Kievs with mashed potatoes, peas and any excess butter poured over.

GARLIC BUTTER

SERVES 4

1 bulb of wet garlic
2 wet or dried garlic cloves, grated
200g unsalted butter, at room temperature
2 wild garlic leaves, finely sliced, and garlic flowers (if you can find them)
2–3 tablespoons chopped parsley
sea salt flakes and freshly ground black pepper

Heat the oven to 200°C/ Gas Mark 6. Wrap the bulb of wet garlic in foil and roast for 40 minutes, or until the cloves are soft and gooey when squished. Leave to cool a little. Place the squeezed-out roasted garlic cloves in a small food processor with the grated garlic, butter, sliced wild garlic leaves, parsley and plenty of salt and pepper and blitz until smooth. If you have managed to get hold of wild garlic flowers, stir them into the garlic butter.

CRISPY CHICKEN, SATAY SAUCE & ASIAN SPIRALIZED VEGETABLE NOODLE SALAD

So now we get to spiralizing vegetables: the art of turning vegetables into 'noodles' with a spiralizer. This is a technique that the Japanese have been using for ages to create garnishes, and one that health freaks are now using as a replacement for noodles. Ultimately, you are eating not noodles but salad. I tested cooking spiralized vegetables in a variety of different styles and discovered that even a second of cooking takes the vegetables a little too far, so the best way to eat them is raw with a hot sauce or, even better, marinated. Here, I've taken classic Malay flavours (chilli, crispy shallots, fresh herbs and peanut sauce) and paired them with a variety of different vegetable noodles and some crispy chicken. The result is a dish that's so damn delicious that even though technically you're not eating noodles, you don't feel like you're missing out.

6 free-range chicken thighs, boned, skin on (if you can't find boned-out chicken thighs with the skin on, it is really easy to take the bones out yourself)
2 tablespoons curry powder
pinch of salt
1 tablespoon coconut or rapeseed oil
Crispy Shallots (see opposite)
lime halves, to serve (optional)

For the vegetable noodles

1 large sweet potato, unpeeled
½ daikon
1 large courgette
3 shallots, finely sliced
a large bunch of mint, leaves picked and roughly chopped
a bunch of coriander, leaves picked and roughly chopped
a bunch of Thai basil leaves (or plain basil if you can't get it), leaves picked and roughly chopped

For the dressing

2 red Thai bird's eye chillies, deseeded if you prefer
juice of 2-3 limes
2 tablespoons fish sauce
1 tablespoon palm sugar
1 teaspoon tamarind paste

You will also need a spiralizer

Put the chicken in a large bowl, add the curry powder and salt and massage the spices and salt into the chicken thighs until they are coated all over. Set aside.

While those flavours are doing their job, use a spiralizer to turn your sweet potato, daikon and courgette into noodles. Put them in a large mixing bowl.

Make the dressing by placing the chillies, lime juice, fish sauce, palm sugar and tamarind paste into a blender and blending well. Pour the dressing on top of the vegetable noodles and mix thoroughly, then place in the fridge until you are ready to serve.

Now make the satay sauce. Heat the oil in a frying pan over a moderate heat, add the curry paste and fry for 2 minutes, or until aromatic. Pour in the coconut milk and chicken stock and then add the peanut butter, sugar, fish sauce, tamarind paste, lime leaves and lime juice. Bring to the boil, then reduce the heat and simmer for about 5 minutes, or until it has reduced and become a richly flavoured satay sauce.

Get a frying pan hot and add the oil. Fry the chicken, skin-side down, for 4–5 minutes, or until golden and crispy. Turn over and cook for another 4–5 minutes, or until the chicken is cooked through. Remove from the pan and leave to rest for a few minutes.

Add the mint, coriander and basil leaves to the noodles and toss together. Transfer the noodle salad to a serving dish. Carve the chicken into slices and place on top. Drizzle over the satay sauce, garnish with the Crispy Shallots and serve with lime halves to squeeze over, if liked.

CRISPY SHALLOTS

SERVES 8
. . . .

4 tablespoons coconut or
  rapeseed oil
4 banana shallots, thinly
  sliced into rings

Heat the oil in a frying pan over a low heat and fry the shallots for 10–15 minutes, or until they start to crisp up and turn a light golden colour. Scoop out the shallots and drain on some kitchen paper.

For the satay sauce

1 tablespoon coconut or
  rapeseed oil
2 heaped tablespoons Thai
  yellow curry paste
200ml coconut milk
200ml fresh White Chicken Stock
  (see page 212)
4 tablespoons crunchy peanut
  butter
2 tablespoons palm or brown
  sugar
1 tablespoon fish sauce
1 teaspoon tamarind paste
4 lime leaves
juice of 1 lime

OOZE

....

RICH & CREAMY

BAKED PORRIDGE

This baked porridge has the same emotional connection for me as a baked rice pudding. It is more of a brunch dish than a breakfast one. I say it's a brunch dish because it's slow-cooked in the oven, ideal for when you can't be asked to sit and watch and stir porridge. It takes almost an hour to cook from start to finish, but it's worth it. In Scotland we would have eaten this pretty plain, made with milk and a spot of salt, then scooped out of the dish and topped with brown sugar and more milk, but here I've made a healthier version that omits the sugar and will put lots of goodness into your body. I make this looser than most baked porridges as I hate stodgy porridge.

Preheat your oven to 200°C/Gas Mark 6 and liberally grease a baking dish with coconut oil.

Pop the oats and oat bran in a large mixing bowl. In a separate bowl or large jug, add the mashed bananas, milk, vanilla extract, sugar or syrup and salt and stir. Pour this mixture over the oats and oat bran and leave to stand for 5 minutes, or until the oats start to absorb the liquid.

Arrange the blueberries and raspberries into the prepared baking dish, pour the porridge mixture over the top and bake for 25 minutes. Sprinkle the flaked almonds over the top, then return to the oven and continue to bake for another 25 minutes, or until golden brown on top. Allow to cool for 5 minutes, then serve with more almond milk if required.

coconut oil, for greasing
200g porridge oats
3 tablespoons oat bran
2 tablespoons coconut sugar
  or maple syrup
½ teaspoon salt
2 bananas, mashed
1 litre milk or almond milk
1 teaspoon vanilla extract
pinch of salt
100g blueberries
100g raspberries
toasted flaked almonds,
  to garnish

POWER PORRIDGE

Porridge is probably the ultimate power food, but it's full of carbohydrates so I wanted to create a lower-carb porridge that still packed a good fibre punch. I've used classic porridge oats as the base (I prefer rolled oats for texture but you can use pinhead oats if you prefer), then added in oat bran for more fibre, and pimped-up the protein factor with quinoa, amaranth flakes and some chia seeds. This is really delicious and takes away the heaviness you sometimes get when you just eat oats.

···

Place the oats, oat bran, quinoa and amaranth flakes and chia seeds in a bowl and mix well, then transfer to a food storage container. Alternatively, you can put the ingredients directly into the container, put the lid on and shake it like crazy until you're sure it's all mixed up. This oat mixture will last for ages in a sealed container. I tend to make a batch of this on a Sunday night to get me through the week.

To make the porridge, place 2 tablespoons of the oat mixture in a saucepan and cover with the milk. You can add a spot of salt at this stage if you like. I really think it needs some salt but some people are funny about that kind of thing so I leave it up to you. Now cook the porridge over a low heat. I like to do this really slowly for about 10–15 minutes. Sometimes it feels like the mixture's not going to absorb all the milk but it does. When it's ready it looks like (I'm sorry for this reference) wallpaper paste: porridge should be a pouring consistency not a dropping-off the spoon one. Spoon the porridge into a bowl, pour over the syrup, and then add the toppings.

For mango, passion fruit and coconut porridge, make the porridge as above, but replace the milk or almond milk with coconut milk or, for a skinnier version, 150ml coconut milk and 150ml coconut water. Top the porridge with the mango, passion fruit seeds and toasted coconut.

100g porridge oats
2 tablespoons oat bran
2 tablespoons quinoa flakes
2 tablespoons amaranth flakes
2 tablespoons chia seeds

Per portion

300ml milk or almond milk
½–1 tablespoon maple or coconut
   blossom syrup
a pinch of salt (optional)

*Peach & berry topping
   (per portion)*

½ peach, chopped
50g mixed berries
1 tablespoon milled seeds and
   flaxseeds

*Mango, passion fruit & coconut
porridge (per portion)*

300ml coconut milk or 150ml
   coconut milk and 150ml
   coconut water
½ ripe but firm mango,
   chopped
seeds of ½ passion fruit
1 tablespoon toasted coconut

MOZZARELLA EN CAROZZA

I can tell you exactly where I was the first time that I had mozzarella en carozza. It was at a family-run restaurant off the Kings Road called La Famiglia. We used to go there pretty much just for the mozzarella en carozza and their lamb chops. It was my sister Cora's favourite. This dish comes in a few guises, mostly floured, egged and then breadcrumbed and served with a tomato and basil or tomato and anchovy sauce, but I like it the way we always used to get it, which was kind of like an 'eggy bread' fried cheese sandwich. So that's how I've done it here.

....

To make the tomato sauce, heat the oil in a small saucepan, add the garlic and basil and fry gently for 1–2 minutes, or until aromatic and softened but not too golden. Pour over the passata, add the vinegar and sugar and cook slowly for about 15 minutes, or until thickened. A good indicator as to whether the sauce is done is when the oil starts to split a little. Season with salt and pepper and blitz in a blender or with an immersion blender to make a smooth sauce. Keep warm.

To make the mozzarella en carozza, cut the crusts off the bread and slice the ball of mozzarella into 4. Using a rolling pin, roll out each slice of bread like pastry until it's really thin. Brush one side of each piece of bread with the egg and then lay a slice of mozzarella in the centre of 4 of the slices. Use the other 4 slices of bread (egged-side down) to cover the mozzarella and make 4 sandwiches. With a 10cm round pastry cutter, cut out the mozzarella sandwich like ravioli. Squeeze the edges of the bread together to seal the edges.

Heat the oil in a large frying pan. Add the butter and once it's melted and foaming lay each of the mozzarella sandwiches in the hot butter. Fry for 1 minute, and then turn over and fry for a further minute on the other side. Repeat this until the sandwiches are crisp and golden on each side. Remove from the pan with a fish slice and drain both sides on kitchen paper, then sprinkle with sea salt.

Divide the sauce between plates, lay a mozzarella en carozza on top and serve piping hot with basil leaves to garnish.

For the tomato sauce

3 tablespoons olive oil
3 garlic cloves, very finely chopped
1 basil sprig, plus a few extra leaves to garnish
400ml passata (I make my own by blending a 400g can of cherry tomatoes)
splash of sherry or red wine vinegar
pinch of caster sugar
sea salt flakes and freshly ground black pepper

For the mozzarella en carozza

8 slices of white bread
1 x 125g ball of mozzarella cheese
2 free-range eggs, beaten
30ml olive oil
1 tablespoon butter

PREPARATION TIME
10 minutes, plus cooling

COOKING TIME
15 minutes

EGG & ONIONS
TO SANDWICH OR NOT TO SANDWICH?

Essentially this recipe is just the best egg mayonnaise filling for a sandwich. Egg and onions are a massive deal in Jewish food, so much so that I had to ask about 20 people how they made theirs and received such different results. Some people made a classic egg mayo and stuffed it with sliced spring onions; some cooked down their onions in schmaltz; others simply used chopped and salted raw white onions. My version is a mixture of the lot: I slowly cook white onions in salted schmaltz, then whip them into an egg mayo and finish with plenty of very thinly sliced spring onion. The person who gave me the biggest insight into the perfect egg and onions was my friend Elly Curshen who runs the Pear Café in Bristol. She makes a sandwich in honour of her Grandma Angela that she sells at the café. Her egg and onions are served in challah bread with gherkins and Little Gem lettuce leaves. I've gone a step further by using gribenes as well, but you can play with the recipe to make it your own.

···

Bring a saucepan of water to the boil. Boil the eggs for 9 minutes, and then transfer them to a bowl of iced water and leave to cool.

Heat the schmaltz in a small frying pan over a low heat. Add the onions and a good pinch of salt and fry for 10–15 minutes, or until the onions have softened but don't have any colour. Leave to cool for 15 minutes.

Once the eggs are cold, peel and grate them on the coarse side of a grater, then put them into a large mixing bowl. Add the mayonnaise, fried onions and spring onions, mix together and season with plenty of salt and pepper.

Serve the egg mixture in a tray with the gribenes on top and the challah bread on the side or make into open sandwiches topped with whichever of the serving ideas you fancy.

Makes 4 sandwiches

free-range eggs (I like to use Cotswold Legbar eggs)
2 tablespoons Schmaltz (see page 216)
2 onions, finely chopped
5 tablespoons mayonnaise
3 spring onions (white and green parts), finely sliced
sea salt flakes and freshly ground black pepper

To serve

8 slices of challah bread
100g Gribenes (see page 216)

And if you fancy pimping it

4 dill pickles, thinly sliced
a few fronds of dill
1 Little Gem lettuce (optional)

AVOCADO PRAWNS WITH KOREAN ROASTED PRAWN OIL MARIE ROSE SAUCE

Making a rich, roasted prawn oil for the base of your mayonnaise gives the sauce a really intense bisque flavour. Otherwise it's just a classic Marie Rose — except it's not because instead of Tabasco sauce I've used Sriracha chilli sauce and instead of cayenne pepper I've used Korean chilli powder, which gives it an Asian tang that I think improves the flavour.

500g cooked small Atlantic prawns, shells on (these will probably have been frozen)
200ml vegetable oil
2 Little Gem lettuces, finely shredded
a good squeeze of lemon juice
2 ripe but firm Hass avocados
1 teaspoon Korean chilli powder, cayenne pepper or regular chilli powder

For the Marie Rose sauce

2 super-fresh, free-range egg yolks (I use Cotswold Legbar or Burford Brown eggs as they have bright egg yolks)
1 teaspoon Dijon mustard
1 tablespoon sherry vinegar
100ml extra virgin olive oil
1 tablespoon lemon juice
2 tablespoons tomato ketchup
1 tablespoon tomato purée
1 teaspoon brandy
2 teaspoons Sriracha chilli sauce
sea salt flakes and freshly ground black pepper

First you need to make your roasted prawn oil. Peel the prawns, keeping the shells to one side and the prawns to the other. Heat the vegetable oil in a saucepan over a medium heat, then add the prawn shells and start to fry them. To begin with a lot of liquid will come out of the shells but this will evaporate and then the prawn shells will begin to fry. Fry for 3–4 minutes, bashing the heads to get all the juice out of the shells, until the prawn shells go lightly golden. Leave to infuse for 20 minutes, then strain through a fine sieve. Discard the shells and leave the roasted prawn oil to cool until it reaches room temperature.

To make the Marie Rose sauce, place the egg yolks, mustard, vinegar and some seasoning in a mixing bowl. Combine the roasted prawn oil with the olive oil in a jug. With an electric hand whisk, beat the egg mixture and very slowly trickle the combined oils into the mixture. It will take a few seconds before the mayonnaise starts to emulsify. Keep trickling in the oil until half of it has been used up, by which stage the mayonnaise should be stable and you can speed up the pour until all the oil is combined and you have a thick, wobbly mayonnaise. Season with the lemon juice, salt and pepper. Add the ketchup, tomato purée, brandy and chilli sauce to the mayonnaise and mix together to make the sauce. It will now be a thick but coatable consistency.

Divide the lettuce between 4 plates and squeeze over some lemon juice. Place half a stoned avocado on the lettuce, squeeze over some lemon juice and sprinkle with a tiny bit of salt. Divide the prawns between the avocados, then spoon over 1–2 tablespoons of the Marie Rose sauce. Sprinkle with a spot of Korean chilli powder and serve.

PREPARATION TIME
10 minutes

COOKING TIME
5–10 minutes

KIMCHEESE CUBAN SANDWICH

This recipe came about by happy accident. I want to say that I created the Kimcheese Cuban Sandwich through a meeting of minds with food writer Diana Henry on Twitter but undoubtedly it had been made before. While testing the carnitas recipe for this book, I ended up with some extra carnitas and thought I'd try my hand at a Korean-inspired Cuban sandwich as I always have kimchi and the rest of these ingredients in my storecupboard. It was a winner! The pairing of kimchi's spicy sourness with melty cheese in a toasty is a thing of dreams: it takes the grilled-cheese sandwich to the next level. If you've never tried this combination, do it right now as a matter of urgency. Make the carnitas. Make sure you have leftovers. Then make this sandwich. You'll thank me...

Heat a large, cast-iron griddle or panini press. Generously butter one side of the sourdough slices or the cut sides of the rolls and toast on the griddle over a moderate heat or in the press for 1–2 minutes, or until lightly browned. Transfer to a work surface and generously brush the buttered sides with mustard. Layer the carnitas or roast pork, Swiss cheese, kimchi, spring onions and pickles on top of the mustard on 2 of the slices of bread or rolls and close the sandwiches.

Generously brush the outsides of the sandwiches with butter and set them on the griddle or press; if using a griddle, top the sandwiches with a large baking sheet and weigh it down with something heavy, like a cast-iron skillet. Toast the sandwiches over a moderate heat on the griddle for 3 minutes per side, or toast for 3 minutes in total in a press, until the sandwiches are browned and crisp on the outside and the cheese is melted. Cut the sandwiches in half and serve piping hot and oozy. Warning: the fillings will dribble all down your face.

plenty of softened butter
2 thick slices of sourdough
  bread or 2 panini rolls or
  baby ciabatta rolls
1 tablespoon French mustard
300g leftover Carnitas (see
  page 130) or roast pork
250g thinly sliced Swiss
  cheese, such as Emmental
100g Gizzi's Kimchi (see page
  217), roughly chopped
2 spring onions, finely chopped
3 half-sour dill-pickled
  cucumbers

SERVES 8
....
PREPARATION TIME
30 minutes, plus soaking,
chilling and resting

COOKING TIME 1¾ hours

WILD MUSHROOM, TRUFFLE & TUNWORTH PIE

Let's look at what we have here: a whole Tunworth cheese (a British soft cheese from Hampshire) set inside a layer of truffled mushrooms wrapped in puff pastry. This is what the French would call a pithivier and we would describe as a posh pasty or pie — I'm going with pie! The whole thing is baked to a perfect golden puff, and when it's ready to eat (alongside a bitter leaf salad) it is the perfect combo of oozy, truffley goodness.

....

Melt the butter in a frying pan over a high heat and fry the chestnut and Portobello mushrooms, in batches if necessary, until they have browned and are softened. Return all the fried mushrooms to the pan, add the porcini mushrooms and fry for a further couple of minutes. Now add the garlic and thyme and cook for another minute or two. Whisk in the flour and let it cook for 1 minute, then whisk in the Madeira and the reserved porcini mushroom stock, bring to the boil and cook until the mixture has thickened to a coating consistency. Stir in the cream, Parmesan, vinegar and truffle oil and season. Leave to cool, then transfer to the fridge until cold. The mushroom filling needs to be cold or the pastry will get warm and be ruined.

Unroll the pastry and place on separate baking sheets lined with parchment paper. Cut out 2 large circles of pastry: one 30cm in diameter and one 35cm in diameter. Discard the trimmings.

Spoon one-third of the cold mushroom mixture on to the smaller pastry circle. Place the Tunworth on top and then cover with the remaining mushroom mixture. Brush egg wash around the outer edge of the pastry. Cover with the larger pastry circle and press lightly to remove any trapped air. Select a bowl that is slightly larger than the dome of the pie and invert it over the pastry. Press down on the bowl to seal the pie edges. With a small sharp knife cut the pastry into a scallop shell shape and discard the trimmings. Brush the top of the pie with egg wash. With a paring knife, cut a pinwheel pattern in the top of the pie, stopping short of the scalloped edge. Chill in the fridge for 30 minutes.

Preheat the oven to 190°C/Gas Mark 5.

Bake the pie for 30 minutes, or until it's golden and the pastry has puffed up. I suggest you leave it to rest for 30 minutes before eating, otherwise the cheese will ooze all over the place.

30g butter
300g chestnut mushrooms, chopped
300g Portobello mushrooms, chopped
25g porcini mushrooms (rehydrated in 500ml boiling water for 1 hour, then drained, reserving the stock)
2 garlic cloves, finely chopped
a few thyme sprigs, leaves picked
30g plain flour, plus extra for dusting
50ml Madeira
100ml double cream
20g Parmesan cheese, grated
1 teaspoon sherry or tarragon vinegar
1–2 teaspoons white truffle oil
2 x 375g packets of ready-rolled all-butter puff pastry
1 Tunworth cheese or Camembert
2 egg yolks, whisked
sea salt flakes and freshly ground black pepper

SERVES 4-6
....

PREPARATION TIME
40 minutes

COOKING TIME
5¾ hours

BRAISED VEAL TAIL WITH SAFFRON RISOTTO & BONE MARROW GREMOLATA

This recipe is based on osso bucco, but instead I've used veal tail. The meat becomes gelatinous from being cooked with marrowbone, and you get to eat the marrow with the dish at the end in a marrow gremolata which enriches the dish, making the whole sticky process even more rich. The saffron risotto is elegant and lifting with an acidulated tang that balances the whole thing out. It's a labour of love in both the sourcing of ingredients and the making, and it's not for the faint-hearted as it's richer than rich. I dread to think what the calorie count would be but it has to be one of the most delicious and satisfying things you can eat. If you want to make life a little bit easier for yourself, you can cook the stew the day before, which will allow all the flavours to emulsify.

....

4 tablespoons olive oil, plus extra to rub over the marrowbones
15g butter
2 veal tails, cut into segments and trimmed of most of the excess fat
2 onions, finely chopped
2 carrots, finely chopped
2 celery sticks, finely chopped
1 teaspoon tomato purée
1 teaspoon plain flour
1 bottle decent white wine
350ml passata
600ml-1 litre fresh Veal or Beef stock (see page 213)
1 bay leaf
a few parsley sprigs
a few thyme sprigs
a few rosemary sprigs
a few celery leaves
4 veal marrowbones, each about 6cm long
sea salt flakes and freshly ground black pepper

Preheat the oven to 150°C/Gas Mark 2.

Heat 2 tablespoons of the oil and the butter in a frying pan. Season the veal tails with plenty of salt and pepper, then add them to the frying pan and brown the meat on all sides, paying particular attention to rendering the fat down. Remove from the pan and set aside.

In a casserole dish that's large enough to hold all the veal, heat the remaining oil. Add the onions, carrots and celery (this mix is called a soffrito in Italian cookery) and cook slowly for 10–15 minutes, or until sweet and softened but not really taking on much colour. Add the tomato purée and ramp up the heat. Fry the vegetables and the purée for 2–3 minutes, or until a little caramelized. Add the flour and cook out for 1 minute. Slowly add in the wine, then add the passata and stock. Add the veal tails to the sauce, along with all the herbs and plenty of freshly ground black pepper. Lay a sheet of damp greaseproof paper over the top of the stew and place the lid firmly on top of the casserole.

Pop in the oven and slowly braise for 4½ hours, or until the meat is falling off the bone. Carefully remove the veal tails from the casserole, wiping away any of the soffrito, and set aside. Strain the sauce through a fine sieve into a saucepan and discard the vegetables and herbs. You should have about 1 litre of liquid left. Cook the sauce to reduce it by about »

For the acidulated butter

1 shallot, finely sliced
75ml dry white wine
75ml white wine vinegar
50g butter

For the risotto

1 tablespoon olive oil
2 shallots, finely sliced
250g risotto rice (I use
  Carnaroli or Arborio)
200ml dry white wine
600ml hot fresh White Chicken
  Stock (see page 212) infused
  with a generous pinch of
  saffron threads
40g Parmesan cheese, grated,
  plus extra to serve
90g mascarpone cheese

For the bone marrow gremolata

small bunch of flat leaf
  parsley, finely chopped
grated rind of 1 lemon
1 garlic clove, finely grated
marrow from 2 of the roasted
  marrowbones
2 tablespoons of the fat from
  the roasted marrowbones
1 tablespoon extra virgin olive
  oil

≪ one third, or until the sauce becomes light, syrupy and glossy. Return the veal to the pan and heat through.

Meanwhile, increase the oven temperature to 220°C/Gas Mark 7 after you have removed the stew from the oven. Rub the marrowbones with oil and season liberally with salt and pepper. Roast the bones for 45 minutes, or until golden brown and the marrow has begun to melt.

To make the acidulated butter, put the shallot, wine and vinegar in a saucepan and reduce until there is only about 1–2 tablespoons of liquid left. Strain the reduction through a sieve into a bowl, then use a small immersion blender or whisk to beat the reduction together with the butter. Chill the acidulated butter in the fridge. You will use this as the base for the risotto.

To make the risotto, heat the oil and half of the acidulated butter in a large sauté pan. Add the shallots and fry for 5–8 minutes, or until softened. Add the rest of the acidulated butter, then add the rice and fry it in the shallot-and-butter base for 1–2 minutes. Turn down the heat to medium, then pour over the wine and stir the risotto continuously until the wine has been absorbed and the rice has started to become creamy. Now, ladleful by ladleful, add the stock, stirring slowly but continuously until each ladleful has been absorbed. If you have cooked the risotto correctly you will have used up the exact amount of stock but if you've cooked it too fast then you may need to add a splash more water. Turn off the heat, top with the Parmesan and mascarpone and rest the rice, covered, for 5 minutes. Remove the lid and stir.

While the risotto is resting, quickly make the gremolata by mixing all the ingredients together in a bowl.

Serve the risotto with a couple of scoops of bone marrow, a couple of pieces of the veal tail, some of the bone marrow gremolata poured over the top and some extra grated Parmesan.

SERVES 8
....

PREPARATION TIME
10 minutes

COOKING TIME
35 minutes

ROASTED BABY CAULIFLOWERS WITH CHEESE SAUCE

This is cauliflower cheese made even better. Roasting the cauliflowers means you don't get that soggy, smelly old-style version; instead, the cauliflowers are sweeter, with a caramelized taste. The perfect cheese sauce and crispy shallots give this dish a more umami flavour and a delicious, sweet-textured crunch. This dish is IDEAL on its own with a salad, but I like to serve it alongside roast beef, Yorkshires, horseradish sauce and bone marrow gravy.

Preheat the oven to 240°C/Gas Mark 9.

Melt the butter in a frying pan. Place the baby cauliflowers in a medium-sized, ovenproof dish. Rub each cauliflower with some of the melted butter, just as you would a roast chicken, and season with salt and pepper. Roast for 20 minutes, or until golden.

Meanwhile, make the cheese sauce. Melt the butter in a saucepan over a medium heat. Add the flour and cook for a few minutes, stirring to form a roux. Gradually whisk in the milk, a little at a time. Add the bay leaf, mustard and spices and cook for 10–15 minutes, or until you have a thickened and smooth sauce. Remove the sauce from the hob, add the cheeses and stir until the cheese is well combined and melted.

Pour the cheese sauce over the roasted cauliflowers and return to the oven to bake for a further 15 minutes, or until golden.

Sprinkle the Crispy Shallots over the cauliflower cheese and serve straightaway.

50g butter
8 baby cauliflowers
Crispy Shallots (see page 79)
sea salt flakes and freshly
  ground black pepper

For the cheese sauce

40g butter
40g plain flour
600ml milk
1 bay leaf
1 rounded teaspoon English
  mustard
grating of nutmeg
a pinch of allspice
a pinch of cayenne pepper
80g Cheddar cheese, grated
80g Parmesan cheese, grated

CHAR

MEATY & GRILLED

GRILLED CAULIFLOWER WITH CURRIED HUMMUS & CASHEW NUT BRITTLE

SERVES 4

....

PREPARATION TIME
20 minutes, plus cooling

COOKING TIME
20 minutes

1 cauliflower, leaves removed
   and carved into stalk
Crispy Shallots (see page 79)

For the curry oil

150ml vegetable oil
handful of curry leaves
1 teaspoon curry powder

For the cashew nut brittle

100g caster sugar
100g cashew nuts, roasted

For the curried hummus

1 teaspoon curry powder
1 x 300g tub of hummus

For the dressing

½ small bunch of coriander
   leaves, finely chopped
1 small red chilli, finely
   chopped
squeeze of lemon juice
sea salt flakes

My friend Ben Denner, who runs burger restaurant Lucky Chip and grill restaurant Licky Chops, blew my mind one day with the simplest barbecued head of broccoli with yogurt and mustard seeds. It was a testament to great ingredients being cooked simply and showed that brassicas take well to a barbecue or griddle pan. So I went away and experimented with some cauliflower and came up with this show-stopper.

....

Bring a medium saucepan of salted water to the boil. Add the cauliflower and poach for 3–4 minutes, or until cooked but still pretty al dente. Drain and then transfer to a bowl of iced water to cool down quickly. Leave for 2 minutes, then drain again and pat dry with kitchen paper.

To make the curry oil, heat the oil in a small saucepan, add the curry leaves and fry for about 2 minutes. Add the curry powder, turn off the heat and leave to infuse until the oil is cold. Strain the oil into a jug and discard the leaves.

To make the cashew nut brittle, make a dry caramel by melting the sugar in a small frying pan over a lowish heat until it becomes a rich golden mahogany colour. Add the cashew nuts and stir quickly, then pour on to parchment paper and leave to cool. When completely cool, use a knife to chop the brittle into 5mm pieces or blitz quickly in a food processor to break up.

To make the curried hummus, pour one-third of the curry oil into a bowl with the curry powder and hummus and mix.

To make the dressing, pour one-third of the curry oil into a bowl with the coriander, chilli and lemon juice, season with salt and mix well.

Light a barbecue or heat up a griddle pan until searingly hot. Cut the cauliflower into 4 through the root and rub the remaining curry oil over the cauliflower. Grill it until golden and charred on all sides.

Divide the hummus between 4 plates and smooth out. Top the hummus with a wedge of cauliflower, drizzle with a little of the dressing, sprinkle over some of the cashew nut brittle and Crispy Shallots and serve.

GRILLED BROCCOLI WITH BURRATA, CHILLI & ALMONDS

One of the first things that I ever cooked without my mother was a recipe from my colleague Dave when I worked at Cold Steel piercing studio. It was broccoli with a dressing of toasted almonds, lemon and good olive oil and it was delicious. The recipe has since evolved and I fry some garlic, chilli and anchovies in the oil. Burrata, if you've not had it before, is similar to mozzarella cheese but enriched in the centre with MORE CREAM — one of the wonders of the food world.

Bring a large saucepan of salted water to the boil. Pop the whole piece of broccoli in the pan and boil for 3 minutes, or until the stem is al dente. Drain, then plunge the broccoli into a bowl of iced water. This will stop it cooking and help it to keep its vibrant green colour. As soon as it's cool, carefully remove from the bowl and drain on kitchen paper.

Heat a griddle pan over a high heat (a barbecue would work brilliantly for this, too). Using a pastry brush, lightly brush the broccoli with a tablespoon of the oil and season with salt and pepper. Griddle the broccoli for 3–4 minutes, or until charred on each side. The char really adds to the flavour so don't be shy about it, though you don't want to completely blacken it. Remove from the pan and leave to cool for 20 minutes.

Meanwhile, you can toast your almonds and make the dressing. Heat 1 tablespoon of oil in a frying pan over a medium heat and add the almonds. Toast them for 1 minute, or until they are pale golden, then remove with a slotted spoon and set aside. Add the garlic and chilli to the frying pan and very slowly fry them for about 1–2 minutes to soften. Add the anchovies and melt them into the oil, then remove from the heat and pour over the lemon juice. Pour the dressing into a bowl and season with plenty of salt and pepper. Leave to cool for 20 minutes.

Break up the burrata and lay it out over the base of a platter. Drizzle with the remaining oil and sprinkle with sea salt. Place the whole half of the broccoli, cut-side up, on top and drizzle with a good couple of tablespoons of the dressing. Finally, sprinkle over the toasted almonds and serve.

½ head of broccoli
3 tablespoons olive oil
3 tablespoons marcona almonds, peeled
2 garlic cloves, finely chopped
1 red chilli, thinly sliced
3–4 salted anchovies in olive oil
1 tablespoon lemon juice
1 x 150g burrata cheese, removed from the fridge a good 30–60 minutes before using
sea salt flakes and freshly ground black pepper

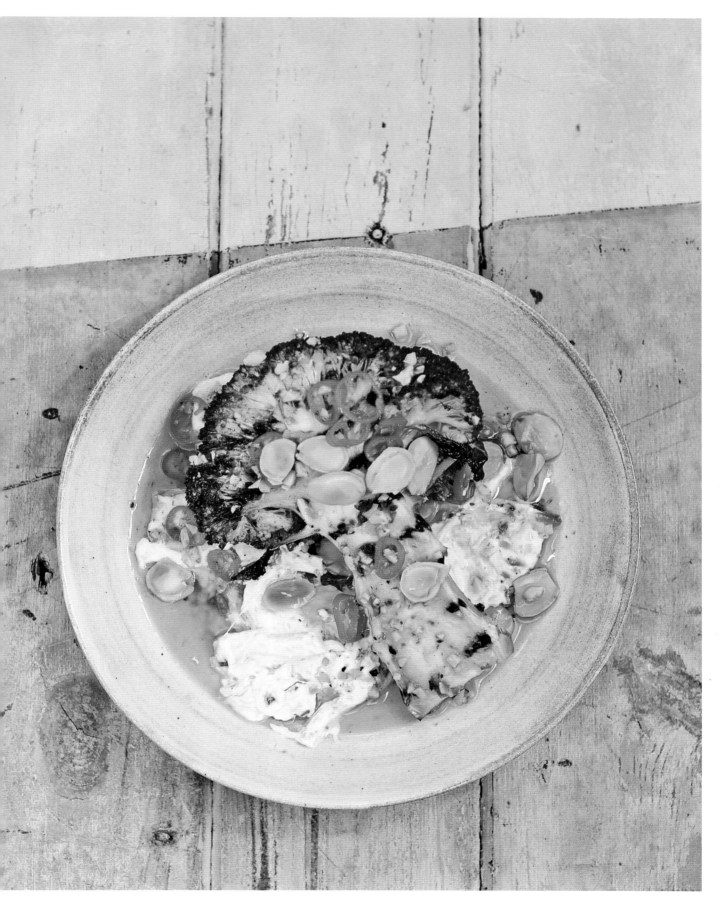

SERVES 6-8
....

PREPARATION TIME
30 minutes, plus curing
(preferably overnight)

COOKING TIME 3½ hours

PORK BELLY BO SSAM WITH SOUPED-UP SSAM JAM

This is the dish that made me fall head-over-heels for Korean food, not in Korea but in New York. I went there to swot up on the best ways of cooking and eating Korean bo ssam, and the best and most original was David Chang's recipe — it had a hint of authenticity, but also some improvements like a pimped-up ssam jam sauce. I've taken his recipe and adapted it by using a smaller and easier-to-work-with cut of meat (pork belly) and then cooking the ssam jam sauce in the pork juices and sticky porkiness that you get at the bottom of the roasting pan. This is a brilliant way to roast meat and serve a roasted joint in a lighter way.

....

6 tablespoons brown sugar
6 tablespoons fine salt, plus
  extra to season the pork skin
2–2.5kg pork belly
150g Gizzi's Kimchi (see page
  217)

*For the souped-up ssam jam
  sauce*

3 tablespoons toasted sesame
  oil
4 tablespoons ssamjang
  (fermented soyabean-and-
  chilli paste)
3 tablespoons rice vinegar
1 tablespoon caster sugar

To serve

Romaine lettuce
cooked sushi rice (about 60g
  per person)
Sesame Spring Onions (see
  opposite)

We are going to start by curing the meat. This will take out all the excess moisture, season the pork belly and give perfect flavour to the meat. To begin with, mix together the sugar and salt in a bowl and then rub the mixture all over the meat EXCEPT for the skin. Then season the pork skin with salt — the salt will allow the skin to crisp up but sugar would stop that. Cover the pork belly with clingfilm and place in the fridge to cure for a minimum of 3 hours but ideally overnight.

Heat your oven to as hot as it will go. For most people, that's 230–240°C/Gas Mark 8–9. Place the pork in a roasting tray and roast for 20 minutes. Lower the oven temperature to 150°C/Gas Mark 2 and roast the pork for 3 hours, or until you can put a fork into the meat and twist it and the flesh pulls apart. Leave to rest for 10 minutes.

While the pork is cooking you can get on with preparing the accompaniments. Start with the ssam jam sauce. Simply mix everything together in a bowl and set aside.

Place the kimchi in a food processor and blitz to a purée. Transfer this to a small serving bowl or dipping bowl.

Once the meat has rested for 10 minutes, transfer the pork to a wooden board while you finish making the ssam jam sauce. Pour out any excess oil from the roasting tray. At the bottom of the tray there will be loads of sticky porky gunge. Pour the prepared ssam jam mixture into the roasting tray, place on the hob and cook over a low heat, stirring and scraping away at the bottom of the tray to pick up all the porkiness, until the sauce has reduced a little. Pour the sauce into a small serving bowl or dipping bowl.

Now you're ready to serve the pork with all the components – the Romaine lettuce leaves, dips and rice. Remove the crackling at the table and use 2 forks to shred the meat. Roll up portions of the pork in the lettuce leaves along with a spot of rice (or you could serve the rice on the side in bowls) and top with the Kimchi, Sesame Spring Onions and ssam jam sauce.

SESAME SPRING ONIONS

5 spring onions (green parts only), very thinly sliced into rings
1-2 hot green chillies, thinly sliced
2 tablespoons toasted sesame oil
¼ teaspoon salt
¼ teaspoon white pepper
½ teaspoon sugar

Simply mix together the spring onions, chillies, sesame oil, salt, white pepper and sugar together in a bowl.

PREPARATION TIME
30 minutes, plus marinating
overnight

COOKING TIME 25 minutes

---

1 leg of lamb, bone out (you can
 ask your butcher to do this)
2 x 300g tubs of hummus
olive oil, for drizzling
50g pine nuts, toasted
6-8 white, brown or granary
 pitta breads, charred,
 to serve

For the marinade

5 tablespoons olive oil
6 rosemary sprigs, leaves
 picked
8 thyme sprigs, leaves picked
a small bunch of mint, leaves
 picked
a small bunch of flat leaf
 parsley, leaves picked
1 bulb of garlic, cloves peeled
1 tablespoon ground cumin
2 teaspoons ground coriander
2 teaspoons paprika
1 teaspoon ground cinnamon
grated rind of 1 lemon

For the pomegranate tabbouleh

250g wholegrain bulgar wheat
2 tablespoons lemon juice
2 tablespoons pomegranate
 molasses
4 tablespoons olive oil
seeds from 1 pomegranate
a small packet (about 30g) of
 flat leaf parsley, leaves
 picked and roughly chopped
a small packet (about 30g) of
 mint, leaves picked and
 roughly chopped
sea salt flakes and freshly
 ground black pepper

LAMB 'SHAWARMA' WITH BURNT PITTAS, HUMMUS & POMEGRANATE TABBOULEH

Strictly speaking, shawarma lamb is the Lebanese version of a doner kebab, which is made by piling up marinated meat on a giant skewer, grilling the outside and then carving it — which is kind of hard to do at home. I have taken the spices, pimped them up and put them into a marinade for a boned-out leg of lamb that is then barbecued medium-rare and served Beiruti-style (on top of hummus) alongside a piquant and punchy pomegranate tabbouleh. This is a terrific, quick and bountifully delicious way to serve a whole roasted joint of lamb.

....

To make the marinade, place the oil, rosemary, thyme, mint, parsley, garlic, spices and lemon rind in a food processor and blitz until smooth.

Open up the leg of lamb and rub it all over with the herby marinade. Cover with clingfilm, place in the fridge and leave to marinate overnight.

You can cook the leg of lamb in one of two ways: either barbecuing the whole thing from start to finish in a barbecue with a lid, or charring the lamb on a griddle and then finishing it in the oven. So here is how you cook it using both methods:

To barbecue the lamb, place a good layer of coal, about palm-length deep, and a couple of igniters in the base of the barbecue and add some wood chips if you fancy. Light the barbecue, making sure the vent at the bottom is just open, and leave until the coals become white-red before cooking. Move the coals to the side of the barbecue to form a semi circle round the edge. When the barbecue is ready, place the leg of lamb over the hot-coal side of the barbecue and lightly char the outside all over. When nicely browned, move the lamb over to the side with no coals and then pop the lid on with the vent only just open. The temperature gauge should come up to between 180°C and 190°C. Smoke-roast the lamb for 20 minutes, turning halfway through, for medium-rare meat. Remove from the barbecue, cover with foil and leave to rest for 15 minutes.

To cook the lamb in a griddle pan and then roast, heat the oven to 220°C/Gas Mark 7. Now heat a griddle pan until smoking. Brown the leg of lamb on all sides on the griddle pan and then place on a roasting tray. Roast for 30–35 minutes, or until medium-rare. Remove from the oven, cover with foil and leave to rest for 15 minutes.

Meanwhile, make the tabbouleh. Cook the bulgar wheat in a saucepan of salted boiling water for 10 minutes, or until perfectly cooked. Drain and leave to steam with the lid on for 5 minutes. Mix together the lemon juice, pomegranate molasses and oil in a bowl with lots of seasoning. While the bulgar wheat is still warm, dress it with half this dressing, then add the pomegranate seeds and chopped herbs and leave to stand for 10 minutes so that the flavours homogenize.

When the lamb is cooked and rested, spread the hummus over a large serving platter. Carve the lamb and place on top of the hummus, then pour over any lamb juices. Drizzle over the olive oil, scatter with the pine nuts and serve alongside the tabbouleh and charred pittas.

VEAL CHOPS WITH SAGE & LEMON BUTTER

Veal is the most delicate of meats in both flavour and its butter-like texture. We don't really eat much of it in this country, mainly because people assume it's unethical, which is a shame. Dairy cows are bred for milk and not for their meat, so the male calves don't have any use – it's a harsh reality of the food chain. A more ethical veal is rose veal; the calf gets time to hang with its mama and even roam around fields in daylight. You should check it out – it's delicious.

Place the butter, garlic, sage, rosemary and lemon rind in a food processor and blitz until you have a smooth herb butter base.

Heat the oil in a frying pan and make sure the frying pan gets really hot. Season the veal chops with plenty of salt and pepper. Lay them in the hot frying pan and fry for 2 minutes on each side, or until they are a good caramelized colour on both sides. Turn down the heat and turn the chops over again on to the side that was first browned. Add a couple of tablespoons of the herb butter. Let the butter melt slowly and tilt the chops to make sure the butter gets underneath them. Slowly cook the chops in the butter for another 1–2 minutes. The butter will make the chops caramelize even more and will add so much flavour to them. Turn the chops over, add 2 more tablespoons of the butter to the pan and finish cooking for another couple of minutes. Veal should be served medium-rare: this will take a bit of time as the chops are quite thick. A good indicator that the chops are cooked is when the meat gets a dewy layer of juice on top when you have turned it over for the final time. Remove the veal from the pan and leave to rest for 5 minutes.

Pour the Marsala wine into the frying pan, stir to deglaze the pan and let it bubble away until it is reduced to a glossy sauce. Once the veal has rested, add any of the meat juices to the pan.

Pour the sauce over the veal and serve. Classically, you would serve this dish with spinach but I also like to bung a small baked potato alongside it.

75g butter
1 garlic clove
15 sage leaves
1 rosemary sprig
grated rind of 1 lemon
1 tablespoon olive oil
2 thick veal chops, about 200g
  each, trimmed
50ml Marsala wine
sea salt flakes and freshly
  ground black pepper

SERVES 2
....

PREPARATION TIME
5–10 minutes, plus marinating

COOKING TIME
10–12 minutes

GREEK SEA BREAM STUFFED WITH LEMON & HERBS WITH FENNEL SALAD

Barbecued fish might be the simplest of dishes but, my god, when it is cooked properly it is one of the nicest things to eat — especially alongside a very thinly sliced fennel salad dressed with lemon juice, good olive oil and fennel friands. The sea bream is best cooked over hot coals but it is also delicious when cooked in a smoking hot griddle pan or under the grill, and there really isn't any difference in timings.

....

Place half the lemon slices and 2 bay leaves inside each fish. In a bowl, mix together the herbs with the oil. Rub the herbs and oil into the fish and leave on a plate to marinate for a couple of hours in the fridge. Mix together the fennel slices and fronds with the oil and lemon juice in a non-reactive bowl and season with salt and pepper. Leave to macerate for 20 minutes.

  Meanwhile, heat your barbecue, griddle or grill. Once hot enough, take the fish out of the fridge and season with plenty of salt and a spot of pepper. Cook the fish for about 5 minutes on each side, or until cooked through. Serve the fennel salad alongside the fish.

1 lemon, thinly sliced
2 sea bream (or sea bass), about 500–600g, ask your fishmonger to gut and scale the fish
4 bay leaves
a few rosemary sprigs, leaves picked and chopped
a few thyme sprigs, leaves picked and chopped
2 tablespoons olive oil
sea salt flakes and freshly ground black pepper

For the fennel salad

2 fennel bulbs, thinly sliced
2 teaspoons extra virgin olive oil
a squeeze of lemon juice

PREPARATION TIME
30 minutes, plus chilling

COOKING TIME
5 minutes

TUNA TATAKI WITH YUZU, GINGER & CRISPY GARLIC

Tataki is a classic Japanese dish of seared beef. The 'tak' is the sound that the meat makes when you sear it. This is my version of the modern classic — made with tuna, yuzu and crispy garlic because tuna loves these flavours. If you make this with beef, use a splash of truffle oil because beef and truffle are fab together.

Season the piece of tuna with salt and pepper, then roll it in the sesame seeds. Set aside.

Heat the oil in a frying pan over a low heat and fry the garlic until it is just starting to colour. The garlic is a very important part of this dish so try not to overcook it: you want it crisp but the garlic will taste burnt if it's even just a little overcooked. Remove the garlic with a slotted spoon and leave to drain on some kitchen paper.

Next, fry the ginger in the same oil until is starts to go a little golden, too. Remove from the pan and set aside with the garlic.

Heat the same pan until it is smoking hot and then fry the block of tuna for 20–30 seconds on each side. You are simply sealing the fish and want it still to be raw in the centre. Remove the tuna from the pan and leave to cool. Once cool, wrap the fish in cling film and pop in the freezer for 2 hours or until firm but still carvable.

Make the ponzu by mixing the soy and yuzu together in a small bowl.

To serve, very thinly carve the tuna. I would use about 10 slices per portion. Arrange the tuna on a serving platter, gently overlapping the fish slices in a long row. Top each slice of fish with a slice of garlic, a few spring onions slices and some of the fried ginger, then finish by topping with some sesame seeds and serve with the Ponzu.

400g tuna fillet (from the tail end for sashimi), trimmed into a block shape

4 tablespoons black or white sesame seeds

5 tablespoons vegetable oil

6 garlic cloves, very thinly sliced

2cm piece of fresh root ginger, peeled and cut into very fine julienne

2 spring onions (green parts only), very thinly sliced into rings

2 tablespoons toasted black and/or white sesame seeds

sea salt flakes and freshly ground black pepper

For the ponzu

3 tablespoons Japanese soy sauce (I love Kikkoman)

3 tablespoons yuzu juice

BURRATA WITH GRILLED PEACH, MELON & PARMA HAM SALAD

Creamy burrata fits in pretty much any place that mozzarella goes. I've been eating the essence of this salad for as long as I can remember. It's evolved for sure, starting as just melon and Parma ham, then adding some good olive oil, then some mozzarella, then making more of a dressing with sherry vinegar and now swapping the mozzarella for burrata and adding grilled peaches. It's a brilliant salad that gets the best out of all its ingredients and will be a hit if you need to whip up something quickly for a summer lunch or as a last-minute starter.

···

Heat a griddle pan over a high heat. Halve the peaches, remove the stones and then cut each half into three pieces. Rub the peaches with a little of the oil and then lay them on the griddle and cook for 2–3 minutes on each side, or until charred. Remove with a metal spatula and transfer to a plate to cool.

Drain the burrata and dry with kitchen paper. Tear up the burrata and spread it over the base of a large serving platter. Next, add the melon slices (I like to do this with no rhyme or reason to it: the more rustic the better). Add the ham slices to the platter, swirled into rosettes. Then, when the peaches are cool enough to touch, add them to the salad and scatter the basil over the top. If you want to be really pernickety, you can lift up some of the burrata to overlap the melon and ham.

Now you need to make the dressing. Place the sherry vinegar in a small bowl with the remaining oil and plenty of seasoning and whisk with a sauce whisk or a fork. Pour this over the salad, finely grind over plenty more black pepper and serve.

3 ripe but firm peaches, flat peaches or nectarines
3 tablespoons extra virgin olive oil
2 x 200g balls of burrata cheese
½ Cantaloupe melon, deseeded, cut into 8–10 thin slices and skin cut off
12 slices Parma ham (or Serrano ham would do nicely)
a small bunch of basil, leaves picked
1 tablespoon sherry vinegar
sea salt flakes and freshly ground black pepper

SOOTHE

SLOW-COOKED FAVOURITES

SERVES 6
....

PREPARATION TIME
20 minutes

COOKING TIME
1 hour

DAK DORI TANG
(KOREAN CHICKEN & POTATO STEW)

My taste buds have changed so much and I crave the heat of chillies so greatly that I'm really not sure if I would prefer a classic chicken casserole instead of this dish. It's a simple chicken stew with English backbone but fiery Korean flavours. The gochujang (Korean chilli paste) and the Korean chilli powder will warm you from the inside out, and the rice wine and rice wine vinegar will add tang.

....

2 onions, 1 cut into quarters and 1 sliced into 8 wedges
6 garlic cloves
3cm piece of fresh root ginger
1 tablespoon vegetable oil
1 whole free-range chicken, skinned and jointed into 10 pieces (you can ask your butcher to do this)
500ml fresh White Chicken Stock (see page 212, or water is fine)
2 rounded tablespoons gochujang (Korean chilli paste)
1 tablespoon tomato purée
3 tablespoons mirin (or use sherry)
1 tablespoon rice wine vinegar
2 tablespoons soy sauce
2 teaspoons sugar
1 teaspoon Korean chilli powder (use any other chilli powder if you can't find it)
500g small new potatoes, peeled
2 carrots, chopped
a bunch of spring onions, each cut into 3 pieces
200g green beans, trimmed and halved
sea salt flakes and white pepper

To serve

cooked sushi rice (about 60g per person)
spring onion, very finely sliced
2 tablespoons white and/or black sesame seeds, toasted

Place the quartered onion, garlic and ginger in a blender with a splash of water and blitz until a smooth paste.

Heat the oil in a large casserole. Season the chicken and fry it in small batches until golden. Remove the chicken from the casserole and set aside. Now fry the onion wedges for 3–4 minutes, stirring and scraping the bottom of the casserole to pick up the chickeny residue, until they are tinged brown and starting to go soft but still hold their shape. Remove the onion wedges from the pan and set aside with the chicken.

Add the onion, garlic and ginger paste to the casserole and fry for 3–4 minutes, stirring constantly, until the paste just starts to turn golden. Pour over the stock, then return the browned chicken and onion wedges to the casserole and add the gochujang, tomato purée, mirin, rice wine vinegar, soy sauce, sugar, chilli powder, potatoes and carrots. Pop the lid on and cook over a medium–low heat for 35 minutes. Add the spring onions and beans and cook, uncovered, for a further 5–10 minutes, or until the chicken is falling off the bone and the potatoes are cooked. If you're worried that the chicken breasts may overcook, remove them after 25 minutes and then return them to the casserole to heat through at the end of the cooking time (but in Korea they wouldn't mind). Serve over sushi rice and scatter with spring onions and toasted sesame seeds.

PREPARATION TIME
30 minutes, plus soaking

COOKING TIME
2 hours

SPANISH CHICKEN STEW WITH CHORIZO, SHERRY & GARBANZO BEANS

Sherry has a bad reputation, doesn't it? It still conjures up thoughts of old ladies at Christmas but in Spain, where sherry originates, it's a whole different ball game and sherries are prized as some of the greatest wines in the world. Sherry is not only delicious to drink, it's also terrific to cook with. Together, sherry, chicken, chorizo and garbanzo beans (the most wonderful Spanish chickpeas, to you and me) make this one damn sexy dish. Stews are best made the day before you need them and it's particularly worth doing so when cooking a stew with beans because it balances out the seasoning and homogenizes. A stew like this benefits from a whole chicken that's cut into pieces. It's weirdly therapeutic and much better both economically and for the environment, but if you are unable to do this you can use 8-10 pieces of chicken thighs on the bone.

···

200g dried garbanzo beans (chickpeas), soaked for 12 hours
2 tablespoons olive oil
1 large free-range chicken, skinned and jointed into 10 pieces (you can ask your butcher to do this)
3 whole raw cooking chorizo sausages, about 240g in total
1 bulb of garlic, cut in half horizontally
2 onions, finely chopped
350ml dry sherry
1 teaspoon sherry vinegar
1 litre fresh White Chicken Stock (see page 212)
a generous pinch of saffron
2 bay leaves
1 rosemary sprig
a few thyme sprigs, leaves picked
a small bunch of flat leaf parsley, chopped
grated rind of ½ lemon
sea salt flakes and freshly ground black pepper

Rinse the garbanzo beans thoroughly and place in a large pan and cover generously with cold water. Cover with a lid and bring to the boil for 25 minutes, or until the outsides feel cooked but the centres still feel a little chalky. They will cook more in the stew.

Preheat the oven to 200°C/Gas Mark 6. I like to cook my stew in stages and fry everything separately in a frying pan before building the stew in a casserole with a lid but if you're worried about too much washing up then you can, by all means, brown everything off straightaway in the casserole. Heat the oil in a frying pan. Season the chicken pieces with salt, then add them to the frying pan, skin-side down, in batches and brown them thoroughly. It's really worth persevering with getting a good caramel colour on the outside of the chicken as this is where all the meaty flavour comes from, plus it will render down all the fat from the skin. Once the chicken pieces are browned, remove them from the frying pan with some tongs and set aside on a plate.

Brown the chorizo all over in the same frying pan, then remove and set aside. I like to cook the chorizo whole in the stew and then slice it afterwards. Next, lay the garlic bulb halves in the frying pan, cut-side down, for a »

« minute, until golden, then remove and set aside.

Now you need to pour away the excess fat from the frying pan (there will be a fair amount) until you are left with about 2 tablespoons of oil. Add the onions and fry them slowly for about 10–12 minutes, until they have softened and have started to tinge golden, then transfer to a casserole. Pour over the sherry, sherry vinegar and stock, add the saffron, bay leaves, rosemary, thyme and half the parsley and bring to the boil. Add the chicken, chorizo, garlic and beans to the casserole. The chicken needs to be 90 per cent immersed in liquid, so top up with more stock to ensure this if necessary. Pop the lid on the casserole and place in the oven for 15 minutes. Turn the oven down to 180°C/Gas Mark 4 and cook for a further 45 minutes.

Now, this is where it gets complicated. This isn't what most people do when cooking stews but it's what they SHOULD do. Remove the casserole from the oven and carefully remove the chicken breast pieces and set aside, leaving the chorizo and chicken thighs and leg meat in the casserole. There will still be a fair amount of liquid in the casserole and the beans will not be fully cooked yet, so pop the casserole on the hob, with the lid off, and cook over a lowish heat for another 15–20 minutes to reduce the sauce, making it taste nice and strong, and until the beans are cooked fully when they are completely tender but still holding their shape. Don't worry about the chicken thighs and leg meat as they are hard to overcook.

Once you're happy with the flavour and thickness of the stew and the beans are cooked through, return the chicken breast pieces to the casserole. Remove from the heat, stir in the remaining parsley and the lemon rind and season to taste. Pop the lid on and leave the stew to rest for 10 minutes. This will make the chicken tender and the beans cooked in a uniform way.

Remove the chorizo from the casserole and slice each sausage into about 10 pieces. Pop the slices back in the casserole and stir through. Spoon a couple of pieces of chicken, some chorizo, beans and sauce on to each plate and serve with a fresh green salad.

OX CHEEK GOULASH

PREPARATION TIME
30 minutes, plus resting

COOKING TIME
4 hours

Beef goulash was never something that I loved or lived for. The stuff we ate when I was growing up had WAY TOO MUCH paprika for me and was thickened with rich double cream. The essence of my goulash is brilliant — and it's a classic. I've used ox cheek, a cut of meat that can be braised really slowly and is full of gelatine so that it cooks into a feathery, sticky, melty braised stew. I've given the goulash more body by adding ale to the braising liquor, added smokiness by using sweet smoked paprika and finished it all off with some soured cream, which is just as it should be. Spätzle (alpine pasta) is so much fun to make and eat, and when fried in butter it is proper rib-sticking comfort food.

2 tablespoons vegetable oil
1kg ox cheek (2 cheeks),
   trimmed and each cheek
   cut in half
2 onions, thinly sliced
6 garlic cloves, peeled
1 tablespoon plain flour
1 teaspoon hot smoked paprika
300ml light or dark ale
500ml fresh Beef or Dark
   Chicken Stock (see page 213)
2 bay leaves
1 tablespoon sweet smoked
   paprika
125ml soured cream
2 tablespoons chopped chives
sea salt flakes and freshly
   ground black pepper

For the spätzle

400g plain flour
50ml milk
100ml sparkling water
3 free-range eggs
a good pinch of nutmeg
30g butter

Heat the oil in a large, heavy-based saucepan. Season the ox cheeks with salt and pepper, then brown all over. Remove from the pan and set aside. Add the onions and fry for 10 minutes, or until softened and golden, adding the garlic for the final minute. Then add the flour and the hot smoked paprika to the onions and stir to coat. Pour in the ale and stir until the sauce thickens, then add the stock. Return the ox cheeks to the pan with the bay leaves, stirring carefully so as not to break up the meat. Pop a lid on the pan and cook on the hob's lowest setting for 3½ hours. The meat is ready when it is cooked through and melting. Add the sweet smoked paprika and season well.

To make the spätzle, mix together all the ingredients apart from the butter in a bowl. Place the batter in the fridge to rest for 10–30 minutes. Bring a large pan of salted water to the boil. Pour the batter into a colander over the pan of boiling water and use a spoon or ladle to force the batter through the holes – this will make wriggly noodles that look like tear drops. Even better, use a spätzle maker if you have one. Poach the spätzle in batches for 1–2 minutes, or until they have set, then remove with a slotted spoon and pop into a bowl of iced water.

Drain the spätzle and heat the butter in a frying pan until it is golden and nutty, then fry the spätzle until they are golden. Serve the spätzle with the goulash and top with soured cream and chopped chives.

PREPARATION TIME
40 minutes

COOKING TIME
3–3¼ hours

FEATHERBLADE BOURGUIGNON

I love a glass of red wine, and if I have the dosh I always go for a good Burgundy over anything else. It is lighter, as a whole, and simply much more refined in flavour. Boeuf Bourguignon is a simple beef and red wine stew. Purists believe that it should be made with a whole bottle of wine and no stock and that the stewing veg should remain in the sauce. It's delicious like this but I like to refine my version by using a featherblade beef cut, which despite stewing will cook to show a bright pink middle and has a mammoth amount of tooth-sucking gelatine in it that makes for sticky, soft, falling-apart meat and a glossy sauce. I do add stock (for an even glossier and stickier sauce) and I strain out the veg, adding in the garnish afterwards for a quick cook while the sauce reduces.

olive oil
4 featherblade beef steaks,
  each about 3cm thick
2 carrots, roughly chopped
1 onion, roughly chopped
1 celery stick, roughly
  chopped, plus a handful of
  celery leaves
1 bulb of garlic, cut in half
  horizontally
1 teaspoon tomato purée
2 teaspoons plain flour
500ml red Burgundy wine
500ml fresh Beef or Veal Stock
  (see page 213)
1 bay leaf
2 rosemary sprigs
4–5 thyme sprigs
4–5 parsley sprigs, plus 1
  tablespoon chopped parsley
150g smoked bacon lardons
12 fresh or frozen baby onions
  or shallots, peeled
100g button mushrooms
sea salt flakes and freshly
  ground black pepper
Perfect Creamy Mash (see page
  128), to serve

Heat a frying pan until it is really hot. Add 1 tablespoon of oil. Season the featherblade steaks with salt and pepper and then fry them for 2–3 minutes on each side to give some pretty slick caramelization to the beef. Remove from the pan and set aside.

Add a spot more oil to the pan if necessary, then add the carrots, onion and celery and fry them over a medium heat for 5–8 minutes, making sure to scrape away at the bottom of the pan with a wooden spoon to remove any meaty bits that have been left behind after frying the steaks; this will add to the flavour. For the final minute, increase the heat and make space for the garlic halves. Fry them until the cut side is golden, making sure to keep the veggies moving around the pan while the garlic is frying. Remove the garlic from the pan and set aside with the steaks.

Now add the tomato purée and fry the veg in the purée; this will caramelize around the veg. Add the flour and stir to coat the vegetables. Cook the flour for 1 minute, then pour over the wine and stock and bring to the boil. Transfer to a medium casserole with a lid. Lower the heat to a simmer, add the steaks, garlic, bay leaf and rosemary, thyme and parsley sprigs to the casserole, cover with the lid and cook on the hob for 2½ hours, or until the steak is starting to fall apart.

Remove the steaks from the stew, being really careful »

« not to let them break up, and lay them on a plate. Now you need to strain out all of the stewing vegetables, so place a sieve over a large bowl and pour the liquor into the sieve. It will be fairly watery with a hint of beefy flavour. Wash out the casserole and then pour the liquor back into it. We now want to reduce the sauce in order to make the flavour really punchy before adding in our garnishes, so put the casserole back on the hob and bring to a gentle simmer over a low heat.

Heat 1 teaspoon of oil in a large frying pan and fry the bacon lardons until the fat has rendered away and the bacon is crisp and golden. Transfer the bacon to the casserole with the sauce. Add the onions to the frying pan and fry them for 3–4 minutes, stirring constantly, until they are golden, then transfer them to the casserole. Finally, add a spot more oil to the frying pan and fry the mushrooms until they are golden. Transfer the mushrooms to the casserole. Return the steaks to the casserole and cook for about 20 minutes, or until the sauce has thickened and is really flavourful and meaty, then season to taste. Serve with Perfect Creamy Mash and choppped parsley.

PERFECT CREAMY MASH

SERVES 6
....

800g potatoes, peeled and cut
  into chunks
150g butter
50ml milk
25ml double cream
a good grating of nutmeg
tons of salt and white pepper

Boil the potatoes in a large pan of salted water for 20 minutes. Drain and leave to steam in a colander until dry, then tip out into a clean pan and mash or crush through a potato ricer until really smooth. With a balloon whisk, whip in the butter, milk, cream and nutmeg over a very low heat until it is piping hot, then season with shed loads of salt and pepper before serving straight away.

CARNITAS WITH GRILLED PINEAPPLE SALSA & PINK PICKLED ONIONS

Making carnitas is a bit like making a stew, although you're roasting the meat in a cast-iron casserole for hours and hours with barely any liquid and relying on the natural juices of the meat and the fat to break it down. Eventually, the liquid evaporates and clings to the meat like a sticky jus and the meat then starts to fry in its own fat. It's INSANELY delicious and a fun alternative to a classic Sunday roast. I've served it with a grilled pineapple salsa (making it very Mexican-Bajan), some avocado and the obligatory pink pickled onions.

·····················

For the carnitas

1kg boned-out pork shoulder, fat and skin on, cut into large chunks
3 tablespoons cooking oil
500ml fresh White Chicken Stock (see page 212)
1 bulb of garlic, cut in half horizontally
2 bay leaves
2 strips of orange rind
2 cinnamon sticks
½ teaspoon coriander seeds
6 sage leaves
3 oregano sprigs
sea salt flakes and freshly ground black pepper

For the pineapple salsa

4 slices of fresh pineapple cut horizontally, each slice 8mm thick
olive oil
½ red onion, finely chopped
1 red chilli, deseeded and finely chopped
2 tablespoons lime juice
a small bunch of coriander, finely chopped

To serve

12 small corn tortillas
Pink Pickled Onions (see opposite)
1 avocado, peeled, stoned and finely chopped, lime squeezed over and sprinkled with salt
good Mexican hot sauce (optional)

To make the carnitas, preheat the oven to 170°C/Gas Mark 3. Season the meat with salt and pepper. Heat the oil in a frying pan, then add the meat in batches and brown well, transferring each batch to a cast-iron casserole once browned. Pour the stock over the meat and then add the rest of the ingredients to the casserole. Pop the lid on and roast for 3 hours, stirring every so often. You will notice that the meat releases a fair amount of liquid. After 3 hours remove the casserole from the oven. The meat will be so soft that you are able to put a spoon through it, and that's EXACTLY what you're going to do. Remove the aromatics and then break the meat up with a spoon. Some bits will be meatier than others. Now return the casserole to the oven, this time with the lid off, and bake for 15 minutes. Remove from the oven, stir to break up more of the meat, then return to the oven and repeat this every 15 minutes for 1 hour. By the end of the cooking time, the liquid will have reduced and the meat will have broken down into soft, feathery, pulled pork pieces and be frying gently in its own fat. You now have carnitas. Season with plenty of salt and pepper.

While the meat is cooking get on with making the accompaniments.

To make the pineapple salsa, heat a griddle pan over a high heat. Rub the pineapple slices with oil and grill them for 2–3 minutes on each side. Transfer to a plate and leave until cool enough to handle, then trim off the skin and remove the core. Slice the pineapple into tiny cubes and place in a bowl. Add the onion, chilli, lime juice, coriander and any pineapple juices that may have been released from the pineapple while it was resting. Give it all a good mix. Leave to macerate for least 20 minutes.

Once the carnitas are cooked, heat up your tortillas in a dry frying pan. Serve all the components on the table and get your pals to help themselves. To build, lay a tortilla on a plate, top with a large spoonful of carnitas and then some pink pickled onions, pineapple salsa and avocado. Add some Mexican hot sauce if you like it spicy.

Any leftover carnitas can be made into the Kimcheese Cuban Sandwich (see page 93).

PINK PICKLED ONIONS

SERVES 4
....

50ml white wine vinegar
30g caster sugar
1 teaspoon salt
1 red onion, thinly sliced

Place the vinegar, sugar and salt in a saucepan and cook over a low heat until they melt together. Bring to the boil for a second and then pour over the sliced red onion in a bowl. Cover with cling film and leave to macerate for at least 2 hours at room temperature before serving.

SERVES 6-8
....

PREPARATION TIME
30 minutes

COOKING TIME
4 hours

BOLOGNESE SAUCE – THE REAL DEAL

This is probably the only recipe that you will ever see me do that hasn't really been tweaked. This is how Bolognese should be made. It's a light sauce made with pork and veal (NOT beef) and has layers of earthy chicken livers and salty, smoky pancetta. It's made with WHITE wine and a slightly unusual reduction of milk and what you get is a ragú that's as rich as it is light and tastes authentic: like one you would get in Italy or at a really good Italian restaurant. The only thing I add is garlic (apparently forbidden), and I stir through a bit of basil after a very long, slow cook. There's definitely more legwork than with your usual Bolognese sauce and it may surpass the weeknight supper bracket but it's worth the effort and ingredients.

....

5 tablespoons light olive oil
400g minced veal or beef
400g minced pork
150g chicken livers, finely
  chopped
150g pancetta, thinly sliced
  and then finely cross-chopped
2 onions, finely chopped
2 carrots, finely chopped
2 celery sticks, finely chopped
6 garlic cloves, finely chopped
200ml milk
1 bottle of white wine
1kg plum tomatoes (I prefer
  jarred to canned), blitzed in
  a food processor
2 tablespoons tomato purée
1-2 bay leaves
6-8 thyme sprigs
2 rosemary sprigs
a good grating of nutmeg
a few basil sprigs, stalks
  and all
sea salt flakes and freshly
  ground black pepper

Heat 2 tablespoons of oil in a large deep casserole over a high heat. Season the mince and chicken livers and then brown the meat in batches. Remove each batch from the casserole with a slotted spoon to drain off the fat and set aside on a plate.

Add the remaining oil to the casserole, lower the heat and fry the pancetta until the fat has rendered away and it has gone golden brown. Add the onions, carrots and celery and cook slowly for 10 minutes, or until they have softened and started to go golden. Add the garlic and cook for a further couple of minutes.

Return the meat to the casserole, pour over the milk and cook for about 5–10 minutes, or until the milk has reduced down. The milk adds a spot of sweetness and also softens the flavours of the acidic alcohol and tomatoes. Pour in the wine and cook for a further 5 minutes before adding the tomatoes, tomato purée, bay leaves and thyme and rosemary sprigs. Cook over a low heat for 3 hours, or until the sauce has reduced but is still very much a pouring consistency and the meat is tender: that is the key to a proper Bolognese; it's a meat sauce.

Remove the herb sprigs from the stew and season with plenty of salt and pepper. To finish, add a grating of nutmeg and stir through the basil sprigs. I serve this with any long pasta, from pappardelle to spaghetti, and tons of freshly grated Parmesan cheese.

....

LASAGNE

My search for the best lasagne recipe has been no mean feat. I always come back to the same philosophy: simply layering the best Bolognese sauce with sheets of fresh pasta, topping it with béchamel sauce and Parmesan cheese and then giving it a long slow bake. Fresh pasta, for me, is a must. It's just as easy to use as dried pasta and can be trimmed with scissors, making it easy to fit the exact size of your dish. Blanching the pasta for a few seconds prior to layering means that it doesn't soak up too much wetness from the sauce, giving the lasagne that desired (sorry for lack of better word) sloppiness. A thick slick of béchamel sauce covered in cheese is better than layers of Bolognese and béchamel and makes the lasagne easier to cut. I love this with a crisp green salad, but there are times when I go back to my teens and serve the lasagne with chips (just don't tell anyone).

½ recipe quantity of Bolognese
  Sauce (see page 134)
200g fresh lasagne sheets,
  blanched for 30 seconds and
  then refreshed in iced water
50g Parmesan cheese, grated

For the béchamel sauce

500ml milk
1 bay leaf
a really generous grating of
  nutmeg
50g butter
50g plain flour
1 x 250–300g ball of mozzarella
  cheese (don't bother with
  buffalo mozzarella as it'll
  get lost in the sauce)
sea salt flakes and freshly
  ground black pepper

To make the béchamel sauce, warm the milk, bay leaf and nutmeg together in a saucepan. Remove from the heat and leave to infuse for 10 minutes, then discard the bay leaf. Melt the butter in a saucepan, then whisk in the flour. Cook the flour for 2 minutes, and then slowly add the infused milk, whisking briskly until combined in order to make sure the sauce remains smooth. Bring the sauce to the boil slowly, making sure you keep scraping the base of the pan. Chop the mozzarella into small cubes and beat it into the sauce, allowing it to melt slowly. Season to taste with salt and pepper and more nutmeg.

Heat the oven to 180°C/Gas Mark 4. Now it's time to build your lasagne. It's easier to do this when the Bolognese and béchamel sauces are both cold but if you're pushed for time it's really not a problem to do it while both sauces are hot. Lay 2–3 lasagne sheets on the base of a 40cm x 20cm ovenproof dish. Add 2–3 ladlesful of Bolognese sauce and smooth down with the back of the ladle. Lay another layer of pasta sheets on top of the sauce and repeat twice more, finishing with a final layer of pasta. Cover the pasta with the béchamel sauce and top this with the Parmesan.

Bake the lasagne for 40 minutes, or until the sides are bubbling and the surface is golden.

PREPARATION TIME
20 minutes, plus cooling

COOKING TIME
1½ hours

NEW YORK-STYLE MEATBALLS & GRAVY WITH COURGETTI

The first time I went to New York I wasn't an annoyingly snobby food brat like I am now. I wanted to try all the classic foods you see in the movies: eat a hot dog or a pretzel from a street-food cart, go to a Jewish deli and visit Little Italy. This desire came from my love of mafia movies and *The Sopranos*, which have so many scenes showing the characters cooking a good tomato sauce – or 'gravy' as it's known by Italian-Americans. In this recipe the tomato 'gravy' is puréed and the meatballs are a tiny bit bigger than we're used to. You can serve them with any long pasta but I've done them here with courgetti (courgettes turned into 'spaghetti' with a spiralizer) that you don't need to cook because the heat of the meatballs and sauce will warm it through.

···

For the meatballs

2 tablespoons olive oil
3 garlic cloves, crushed
1 onion, finely chopped
450g minced pork
450g minced beef
a few thyme sprigs
2 rosemary sprigs
sea salt flakes and freshly
  ground black pepper

For the tomato sauce

1 tablespoon olive oil
3 onions, finely chopped
2 garlic cloves, crushed
1 tablespoon tomato purée
1 x 400g can chopped tomatoes
1kg fresh plum or cherry
  tomatoes, chopped
1–2 tablespoons red wine or
  sherry vinegar
1 teaspoon sugar
½ bunch of basil

To serve

100g courgetti per person, or
  cooked pasta
grated Parmesan cheese

To make the meatballs, heat 1 tablespoon of olive oil in a saucepan, then add the garlic and onion and sweat for 4–5 minutes, or until soft and a little golden. Leave to cool. In a bowl, mix together the minced pork and beef with the sweated onion and garlic and the herbs and season well with salt and pepper. Fry a tiny bit of the meatball mixture and then taste to check the seasoning. If necessary, adjust the seasoning of the meatball mixture. Divide the mixture into 18 round balls (about 80g each) and refrigerate until needed.

To make the sauce, heat the oil in a medium saucepan and sweat the onions for 10 minutes, or until soft, adding in the garlic for the last minute. Stir in the tomato purée and cook for few minutes, then add the canned tomatoes and the plum or cherry tomatoes, vinegar and sugar. Cook the sauce slowly for about 1 hour, or until reduced but still a pouring consistency. At this stage, I like to blitz the sauce in a food processor for an Italian-American-style 'gravy' but you don't have to. Return the sauce to the pan, stir through the basil and season to taste.

While the sauce is cooking, fry off the meatballs in the remaining oil in a heavy-based frying pan until they are browned and cooked through. Add the meatballs to the 'gravy' and cook for a further 10 minutes.

Serve the meatballs and sauce with courgetti and tons of black pepper and grated Parmesan cheese.

PREPARATION TIME
40 minutes, plus cooling
(preferably overnight)

COOKING TIME 4 hours

MERGUEZ SHEPHERD'S PIE WITH CAULIFLOWER MASH

Shepherd's pie is one of my death row dinners. My mum's shepherd's pie is better than your mum's — fact! I almost didn't want to mess with the recipe but my sidekick, Sofia, uses merguez sausages to make a really great version that is spicy, rich and sticky. The cauliflower mash is lower in carbs and is superior to mashed potatoes as a topping.

....

2 tablespoons olive oil, plus extra for drizzling
1kg boned-out lamb shoulder, cut into chunks
4 onions, finely chopped
2 carrots, roughly chopped
1 leek, roughly chopped
1 bulb of garlic, cut in half horizontally
1 teaspoon tomato purée
1 tablespoon plain flour
400ml white wine
1 litre fresh Dark Chicken or Beef Stock (see page 213)
1 teaspoon ras-el-hanout
a few thyme sprigs, leaves picked
3 rosemary sprigs, leaves picked and finely chopped
1 bay leaf
8 merguez sausages
sea salt flakes and freshly ground black pepper

For the cauliflower mash

1 large cauliflower, about 900g, broken into florets
2 tablespoons butter
50ml fresh Vegetable or Chicken Stock (see pages 212-13)

You need to start by braising the lamb. Heat 1 tablespoon of oil in a frying pan over a lowish heat. Season the lamb well and fry it in batches until well browned on all sides, then remove the meat from the pan and set aside. Cooking the lamb in batches, leaving space around each piece of meat, means that you get much better colour on the meat, rather than letting it sweat in its own juices. You won't need to add any extra oil to the pan as the lamb has tons of fat in it. Once all the lamb has browned you should have about 2 tablespoons of fat left in the pan.

Lower the heat, add the onions, carrots and leek and cook for 10–25 minutes, or until softened, then lay the garlic, cut-side down, in the pan for a minute until golden. Remove the garlic bulb and set aside with the lamb. Add the tomato purée to the pan with the vegetables, increase the temperature and quickly caramelize the vegetables in the tomato purée. Add the flour and cook for a further minute. Pour over the wine and whisk together.

Transfer the meat, garlic and vegetables to a lidded casserole dish, add the stock, ras-el-hanout and herbs and simmer over a medium-low heat for 2 hours.

After the casserole has been cooking for an hour, heat a frying pan and add the remaining oil. Squeeze the merguez sausages out of their skins and fry them, as if they were mince, over a high heat until browned. Add to the casserole and continue cooking for the remaining hour, until your stew is rich and sticky and the meat is falling to bits. Season with salt and pepper and allow to cool. It's always best to allow a stew to chill completely to at least room temperature before trying to pile the mash on top, so I like to make mine the day before, which »

« gives all the flavours time to harmonize together.

To make the cauliflower mash, roughly blitz the cauliflower in a food processor. Add the cauliflower to a large saucepan with the butter and stock, pop a lid on the pan and cook slowly or 'sweat' for 8 minutes, or until the cauliflower is cooked through. Blitz in a food processor, adding a spot more stock if it needs it, until the cauliflower resembles pomme purée.

Heat the oven to 200°C/Gas Mark 6. Put the stew in a shallow oveproof dish, top the stew with the cauliflower mash and bake for 25 minutes, or until golden and piping hot. Drizzle with olive oil and serve.

SERVES 4

....

PREPARATION TIME
25 minutes

COOKING TIME
30 minutes

FISH STEW WITH FENNEL, SAFFRON & ORZO

The secret to a good fish stew is to use really fresh fish and really good stock. As with a good beef stew, you want your stock to leave your lips sticking together and I always make my own fish stock (see page 213). As for the fish, use what you can. I like a fish that keeps its shape, like monkfish. Everything else about this stew is simple, using flavours that marry well with the fish.

....

1 litre Fish Stock (see page 213) or good-quality shellfish stock

a generous pinch of saffron threads

30ml olive oil

1 fennel bulb, very finely chopped, and fronds picked and stored in iced water

6 garlic cloves, finely chopped

½ teaspoon crushed dried chillies

400g plum tomatoes (I like mine from a jar), blitzed to a purée (or you could use passata instead)

250ml dry white wine

85g orzo pasta

4 large monkfish cheeks or 500g monkfish or any other firm fish that's good for stewing

12 raw king prawns, peeled (keep the shells for stock)

1 squid, cleaned, slashed and cut into bite-sized pieces

2 handfuls of small clams, scrubbed clean and discarding any clams that are chipped or open

a small bunch of parsley, finely chopped

grated rind of 1 lemon

sea salt flakes and freshly ground black pepper

Before you start to cook the stew properly, heat up the stock in a saucepan until it just begins to boil. Add the saffron, reduce the heat and simmer for 1 minute, then turn off the heat. Leave the stock to infuse with the saffron while you get on with the rest of the dish.

Heat the oil in a large casserole with a lid. Add the fennel and fry gently for 5 minutes, or until softened and just starting to turn golden. Now add the garlic and chillies and continue to fry for another 2 minutes, or until the garlic and chillies are aromatic. Pour over the puréed tomatoes and slowly cook for 10 minutes, or until the tomatoes are pretty thick. Pour over the wine and cook for 1 minute, then pour in the saffron stock. Bring the stew, which will now be fairly soupy, to a slow simmer and cook for 10 minutes. You're trying to make a really intense main base flavour, so taste the stew as it's reducing and continue to reduce until you're happy with the flavour, bearing in mind that the sauce will thicken up when you put the orzo and fish into it. And that's exactly what you're going to do next, but in stages.

First add the orzo and a little salt. Orzo takes about 8–10 minutes to cook, so timing is now of the essence. After about 4 minutes you can add the firm fish to the casserole. Continue to cook for 3 minutes, then add the prawns. After another minute the squid can go in. And after about 30 seconds you can add the clams. Now cover and cook for a further 1–2 minutes, or until all the clamshells have opened (discard any that remain closed) and the fish is cooked through. Add the parsley and lemon rind and season with salt and pepper but do taste before salting as the clams can be quite salty. Transfer the stew to a serving dish and top with the fennel fronds.

SAVOUR

....

TASTY MAINS

PREPARATION TIME
20 minutes, plus soaking
overnight

COOKING TIME 1¾ hours

GIGANTES WITH EGGS, YOGURT & HOT CHILLI BUTTER

This is my version of Greek fasolia gigantes, which are tomato-braised butter beans. I use fresh tomatoes and cook the beans in two stages, first getting them almost cooked and then braising them in a tomato sauce with oregano. I serve these beans as a brunch or light supper dish with poached eggs, garlicky yogurt, fresh herbs and hot chilli butter.

....

Soak the beans in cold water overnight. Drain and rinse them in a colander. Put the beans in a large saucepan, cover with plenty of cold water (no salt), and boil for 50–60 minutes, or until they are cooked but still a little firm in the centres.

Meanwhile, in a large casserole dish, heat the olive oil over a medium-low heat and fry the onions for 10–15 minutes, or until really softened and sweet and going slightly golden. Add the garlic and cook for a further 2–3 minutes, then add 2–3 oregano sprigs and the dried chilli flakes and cook out for another minute. Add the tomatoes, vinegar and some black pepper and cook slowly for 20 minutes, or until the sauce has homogenized. Transfer the sauce to a food processor or blender and blitz until smooth, then return to the same casserole. You don't have to blitz the sauce but it does turn this into a much more refined dish.

Drain the par-cooked beans, add them to the casserole with remaining oregano sprigs and cook, partly covered, for 40 minutes, or until the beans are completely cooked.

For the garlicky yogurt, mix together the yogurt and garlic in a small bowl and and season well.

Bring a saucepan of salted water to the boil. Poach the eggs for 3 minutes so that the yolks are still soft. Remove each poached egg with a slotted spoon and drain on kitchen paper.

While the eggs are poaching, make the hot chilli butter. Heat a frying pan over a high heat, add the butter and chilli powder and cook until the butter starts to go slightly brown and nutty. Carefully add the lemon juice, watching out as it will splutter.

Divide the beans between 4 plates and top each with a poached egg and some of the garlicky yogurt. Drizzle over the hot chilli butter to serve.

4 free-range eggs (I use
  Cotswold Legbar or Burford
  Brown eggs as they have
  bright egg yolks)
sea salt flakes and freshly
  ground black pepper

For the beans

300g Greek fasolia gigantes
  or butter beans
100ml olive oil
2 onions, finely chopped
1 bulb of garlic, cloves peeled
  and finely chopped
6–7 oregano sprigs
a good pinch of dried chilli
  flakes
700g fresh vine-ripened
  tomatoes, chopped
1 tablespoon red wine or sherry
  vinegar

For the garlicky yogurt

250g Greek yogurt
2 garlic cloves, grated

For the hot chilli butter

100g butter
1 teaspoon hot chilli powder
squeeze of lemon juice

BAKED HALOUMI WITH TAPENADE

Haloumi is the cheese for which even meat-lovers are happy to ditch their meat quota. I guess it's because you can cook haloumi, and it has texture and real bite. It's also salty and takes on flavour very well. We're used to seeing haloumi that's been grilled or pan-fried in slices but my friend Nice gave me a brilliant technique for ramming extra flavour into it: marinate your haloumi and then slowly bake it. Prepared this way the haloumi is permeated with herby, lemony flavour and cooked to the point of almost being goo – but as we know haloumi won't quite go to goo. It's blooming delicious, especially served alongside a tomato and tapenade salad.

···

2 rosemary sprigs
1 tablespoon thyme leaves
a handful of basil leaves
a small handful of flat leaf
  parsley
2 oregano sprigs
grated rind and juice
  of 1 lemon
1 tablespoon olive oil
1 x 250g block of haloumi
  cheese
sea salt flakes and freshly
  ground black pepper
lemon wedges, to serve

For the tapenade

200g pitted black olives
1 garlic clove
2 salted anchovy fillets in oil
1 tablespoon chopped flat leaf
  parsley
1 rosemary sprig, chopped
50ml olive oil

For the tomato salad

3 vine-ripened tomatoes
2 teaspoons sherry vinegar
2 tablespoons olive oil
a small bunch of basil

Place the herbs, lemon rind and juice and oil in a small blender and blitz until they form a smooth paste. Alternatively, you can finely chop all the herbs and mix the ingredients together in a bowl. Smear the paste all over the haloumi and season with ground black pepper (definitely don't season with salt as the haloumi is salty enough). Cover with cling film, pop into the fridge and leave to marinate for a minimum of 2 hours; it is actually better to let it marinate overnight.

To make the tapenade, simply pop all the ingredients into a small food processor and blitz until blended.

Preheat the oven to 200°C/Gas Mark 6. Lay 2 sheets of baking paper on to a kitchen surface. Place the haloumi and its marinade in the centre of the paper. Fold the paper up over the haloumi and then fold up the edges as if you were making a Cornish pasty. I use paperclips or staples to seal the parcel together as you need it to be as airtight as possible. Pop into the oven and bake for 35–40 minutes. This sounds like a long time but you want the whole block of haloumi to be cooked through.

Meanwhile, make the tomato salad by slicing the tomatoes and laying them on a plate. Season with salt and pepper and then drizzle over the vinegar and oil. Finally, drizzle over 2 tablespoons of the tapenade and finish with a scattering of basil leaves.

Serve the haloumi alongside the salad with extra tapenade to dollop and lemon wedges to squeeze over.

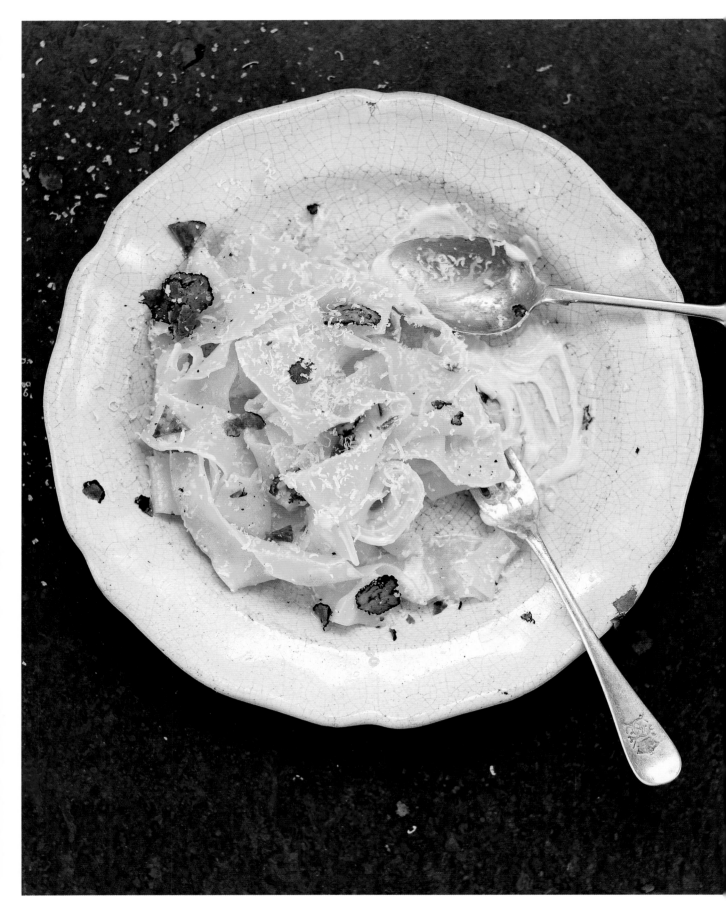

ACCIDENTAL TRUFFLE PAPPARDELLE

You know when something great happens completely by mistake? Well, I was developing a recipe for a truffle béarnaise sauce to go with steak and it was good, great in fact, but I had tons of leftover sauce. My mum and I were chatting about how much we love truffles, what they go well with and how I make my favourite truffle tagliatelli dish (really simply with a butter emulsion sauce that emulsifies with the pasta water, butter and truffle), when suddenly we both slapped our foreheads at the same time, ran into the kitchen and put some pasta on to cook (all we had was pappardelle). We mixed the hot pasta through the warm truffle béarnaise, topped it with more shaved truffle and some Parmesan, devoured it in seconds and then did high-kicks around the house because it was so brilliant. So here I give you my accidental truffle pappardelle.

···

Take your hollandaise sauce and stir in the Parmesan, truffle paste and truffle oil. Allow the sauce to cool a little – it should be warm but not quite room temperature.

Bring a large pan of salted water to the boil and cook the pasta according to the packet instructions until al dente. Drain the pasta and then add it to the truffle béarnaise sauce (remember, the sauce should be warm but not hot) and toss through. Serve straightaway with more grated Parmesan and some freshly shaved truffle if you have the bucks.

Hollandaise Sauce (see
  page 215)
15g Parmesan cheese, grated,
  plus extra to serve
1 teaspoon white truffle paste
1 teaspoon truffle oil (or more
  if you think it needs it)
320g fresh pappardelle
freshly shaved truffle
  (if you fancy it or have the
  cash for it)

VONGOLE WITH BLACK SPAGHETTI & N'DUJA

You know when you're asked about your dream ingredient? Mine has to be clams. I can eat them by the bucket-load. Making a classic vongole and melting in n'duja or sobrasada (heavily cured, spiced spreadable sausages a bit like chorizo) makes this dish extra spicy and porky, and its fluorescent orange oil soaks into the black squid-ink spaghetti a treat.

400g dried black squid-ink spaghetti
1kg small clams (check with your fishmonger that they're from sustainable sources), scrubbed clean and discarding any clams that are chipped or open
50ml extra virgin olive oil
5 garlic cloves, very thinly sliced
1 small dried chilli, finely chopped
150g n'duja or sobrasada sausage
300ml white wine
a generous squeeze of lemon juice
a small bunch of flat leaf parsley
sea salt flakes and freshly ground black pepper

Cook the spaghetti according to the packet instructions in a saucepan of heavily salted boiling water until al dente.

Meanwhile, place a large saucepan with a lid over on a high heat and let it heat up. Carefully (so not to damage any of the shells) tip the clams into the pan with a splash of water. Put the lid on and let the clams steam in their shells for 1–2 minutes, or until they have all opened (discard any that remain closed). Pour the clams into a sieve over a bowl to collect the cooking liquor.

Quickly wash the saucepan you used to cook the clams. Heat the oil in the clean saucepan over a medium heat, then add the garlic and chilli and fry for 2–3 minutes, or until the garlic starts to colour. Add the n'duja or sobrasada and fry until it has completely melted and is starting to get a tiny bit of colour. Pour over the white wine and then carefully pour in the clam cooking liquor, making sure to hold back any sand that may have collected at the bottom of the bowl. Cook until this has reduced by half or until it has become 'saucey'.

While the sauce is reducing, remove the clams from half of the shells (discarding the empty shells). It is a good idea to do this because you need the clam meat but sometimes there are way too many shells for you to be able to mix the whole thing properly. Add the clams (both shelled and unshelled) to the sauce and give a good stir.

Drain the spaghetti, holding back about 1 tablespoon of the cooking water. Add the pasta to the sauce with the cooking water and clams. Squeeze in the lemon and add the parsley, then thoroughly toss the whole thing together. Season with salt and pepper if it needs it – the clams are very salty – and serve piping hot. Don't forget to serve with finger bowls and a bowl for the empty clamshells.

SERVES 2
....

PREPARATION TIME
15 minutes

COOKING TIME
45 minutes

ARRABIATA WITH SARDINES & PANGRATTATO

Storecupboard dinners don't get better than this. *Said in my best Gregg Wallace voice.* And it's true – just because something is not made with entirely fresh ingredients doesn't mean it's bad quality. In fact, I couldn't make this better with fresh stuff. Really great anchovies, olive oil, jarred plum tomatoes, olives and even the jarred sardines are what make this dish taste so good and the pangrattato (poor man's Parmesan) is a brilliant way to use up leftover bread. This simple tomato sauce needs a slow cook to get the right sweetness from the tomatoes.

....

drizzle of oil
5–6 garlic cloves, finely chopped
1 rosemary sprig
½ teaspoon dried chillies, crushed
4 salted anchovies in oil
200ml white wine
650g great-quality plum tomatoes (I like to use jarred rather than canned tomatoes but by all means use canned), whizzed into a purée
handful of basil leaves, plus extra to garnish
100g purple olives, pitted
pinch of sugar (optional)
1 x 300g jar or can of best-quality sardines
180g long thin pasta, such as linguine, spaghetti or bucatini
sea salt flakes and freshly ground black pepper

For the pangrattato

30g olive oil
2 garlic cloves, bashed
1 slice of bread, crusts removed and blended into crumbs in a food processor
grated rind of ½ lemon

Make the pangrattato. Heat the oil and garlic in a frying pan over a medium heat and fry until the garlic is tinged golden brown. Remove the garlic from the pan and discard. Add the breadcrumbs and lemon rind and slowly toast the crumbs over a low heat until they turn a faint golden brown. Remove from the heat, drain on kitchen paper and set aside for later.

Heat a drizzle of oil in a large saucepan and gently cook the garlic and rosemary for 2–3 minutes. Remove the rosemary and discard. Add the chillies and anchovies and cook until the anchovies melt into the oil. Pour in the white wine and puréed tomatoes, stir in half the basil, cover and simmer over a medium heat for 20 minutes. Add the olives and cook for a further 10 minutes, or until the sauce has reduced and thickened. Season to taste with salt and pepper and add a pinch of sugar if necessary. Remove from the heat, lay the sardine fillets on top of the pasta sauce, cover with a lid and leave to warm through for 3 minutes. Don't stir the sardines through the sauce as it's nice to have the whole fish on top of the dish. I try to keep one side silver as it's pretty.

Cook the pasta in a large saucepan of salted boiling water for 1 minute less than the packet's suggested cooking time, or until al dente. Drain the pasta.

Carefully remove the sardines from the sauce. Stir the pasta and the remaining basil through the sauce. Divide between 2 plates and serve topped with a few sardine fillets, a tablespoon of the pangrattato and extra basil leaves.

SMOKED MACKEREL & CAULIFLOWER RICE KEDGEREE

3 tablespoons oil (I use
  coconut oil and it works
  really well)
2 onions, 1½ thinly sliced and
  ½ chopped
3–4 garlic cloves, chopped
3cm piece of fresh root ginger,
  peeled and chopped
1 red chilli (deseeded if you
  don't want it to be too
  spicy), finely chopped
½ teaspoon ground turmeric
½ teaspoon ground cumin
½ teaspoon ground coriander
pinch of ground cloves or
  1 clove
2 free-range eggs (I use
  Cotswold Legbar or Burford
  Brown eggs because they have
  bright orange yolks)
1 small cauliflower, about
  300g, cut into chunks
250ml fresh White Chicken Stock
  (see page 212)
2 smoked mackerel fillets
a small bunch of fresh
  coriander, roughly chopped
½ small bunch of mint, leaves
  picked and roughly chopped
½ tablespoon fresh lemon juice
2 tablespoons flaked almonds,
  toasted
sea salt flakes and freshly
  ground black pepper

To serve

Greek yogurt
lemon wedges

Now that I've gone potty over cauliflower rice (see page 214) I am looking for ways to incorporate it into recipes. My first step was to look at which things go with cauliflower, then other rice dishes. So, here we go: cauliflower is brilliant with curry, with smoked fish and with eggs (among other things), so one rice dish that was glaringly obvious to try was kedgeree. And my god, cauliflower rice makes a brilliant one. I'm still genuinely flabbergasted by cauliflower rice: how filling, quick to cook and genuinely deelish it is. I could shout about it all day long. My kedgeree simplifies everything and is made with ingredients you can get everywhere.

You will need 2 pans: a frying pan and either a sauté pan or a wok with a lid. Heat 1 tablespoon of oil in the frying pan. Add the thinly sliced onions and cook over a very low heat for 15 minutes, until the onions become caramelized and faintly crisp. Drain on kitchen paper and set aside.

While the onions are cooking, you need to make your curry paste. Put the chopped onion, garlic, ginger, chilli and spices in a food processor and blitz until they form a paste. Heat the remaining oil in a sauté pan or wok. When it is hot, add the paste and cook for 5 minutes over a lowish heat until is has completely softened, started to turn golden and lost its liquid content.

Bring a small saucepan of boiling water to the boil. Add the eggs and boil them for 6 minutes. Drain and then place under cold running water to stop the eggs cooking. Peel the eggs and set aside.

Meanwhile, put the cauliflower into the food processor (I don't bother cleaning it after making the curry paste) and blitz it on the pulse setting until it resembles something the size of large couscous.

Once the curry paste has cooked, add the cauliflower to the paste in the sauté pan or wok. Stir-fry over a high heat for 2 minutes, or until each cauliflower grain is coated. Pour over the chicken stock and add a pinch of salt. Stir and then pop a lid on top and cook for 4 minutes. Lay the mackerel, skin-side up, on top, press it down gently so the fish is immersed into the 'rice', then pop the lid back on and cook for another 3 minutes over a lowish heat.

Remove the lid and continue to cook to let some of that liquid reduce. You can peel the skin off the mackerel while this is happening. When there is only about 2 tablespoons of liquid left in the pan and the 'rice' is tender, remove from the heat. Add one-third of the caramelized onions, the coriander and mint (saving a tiny bit for a garnish), and the lemon juice and mix well. Season well. You can break the mackerel up into the kedgeree, if you like, or serve it on top.

Divide between 2 plates. Scatter over the almonds and then the remaining caramelized onions. Cut the eggs in half (they should have slightly gooey middles) and then place 2 egg halves on top of each serving. Garnish with the remaining herbs and serve with Greek yogurt and lemon wedges.

PREPARATION TIME
25 minutes, plus proving
overnight

COOKING TIME 30 minutes

ROASTED FENNEL &
SAUSAGE CALZONE

What's not to love about calzone? It's essentially a pizza that's been folded and made into a Cornish pasty but it's stuffed double-full of filling. Making your own pizza dough is a pain in the bum and I'm not one of those chefs who's going to say otherwise. Making dough is therapeutic, for sure, but it takes ages to rise, it's hard to know when it's the right consistency and it can be temperamental. I suggest you make the dough the day before and let it rise slowly in the fridge, which means you'll only need to make the fillings and bake the calzone on the day. So let's get chatting about this particular calzone. All the greats are in it: the fennel bulbs, seeds and fronds are utter sex when paired with the pork and spice from the fresh sausages and cured pepperoni. This alone makes the whole process worthwhile.

....

2 large fennel bulbs, thinly
  sliced, fronds reserved
1 tablespoon sherry vinegar
  (red or white wine vinegar
  would also be great)
3 tablespoons olive oil
3 sausages (I use Italian
  fennel ones but you could use
  any herby sausages)
150g mozzarella cheese
80g pepperoni or cured fennel
  salami, sliced
a good pinch of fennel seeds,
  toasted
a good pinch of dried chilli
  flakes
sea salt flakes and freshly
  ground black pepper

For the dough

300g strong white bread flour
  or Italian '00' flour
7g sachet of fast-action dried
  yeast
1 tablespoon sugar
100ml lukewarm water
1 tablespoon salt
30ml olive oil

For the tomato sauce

3 tablespoons olive oil
3 garlic cloves, very finely
  chopped
1 basil sprig
400ml passata (I make my own by
  blending a 400g can of cherry
  tomatoes)
a splash of sherry or red wine
  vinegar
pinch of sugar

The day before you want to cook the calzone, make the dough. Add the flour, yeast and sugar to a large bowl, stir well and slowly mix in the water, salt and oil. Knead the dough well for 10 minutes. You can do this in a free-standing mixer with a dough hook for ease. Place the dough in an oiled bowl, cover tightly with cling film, followed by a warm, damp cloth and leave to rise for 2 hours. Knock the dough back, then cover the bowl with oiled cling film and leave in the fridge overnight. This is actually a better way to rise dough, giving it first a fast rise and then a slow one; it allows the yeast to mellow a bit so that the dough doesn't taste so yeasty.

To make the tomato sauce, heat the oil in a small saucepan, add the garlic and basil and fry gently for 1–2 minutes, or until aromatic and softened but not going too golden. Pour over the passata, vinegar and sugar and cook slowly for about 15 minutes, or until thickened. A good indication that the sauce is ready is when the oil starts to split a little. Season with salt and pepper and blitz in a blender or with an immersion blender to make a smooth sauce.

Meanwhile, heat your oven to as hot as it will go. My oven goes up to 250°C but some only go to 220°C/Gas Mark 7. Place the fennel in roasting tray and add the vinegar, 2 tablespoons of oil and some seasoning. Roast for about »

« 20 minutes, turning halfway through, until the fennel is cooked all the way through and tinged golden at the edges. Remove from the oven and set aside until it is cool enough to touch.

Heat the remaining oil in a frying pan. Squeeze the sausages out of their skins, breaking some bits into small meatball-sized pieces and some into larger pieces. Fry the sausage meat for 2–3 minutes, or until cooked through and browned.

Divide the dough into 2 balls. Place each ball on a large sheet of parchment paper and roll it out thinly until it forms a circle about 30cm in diameter. Top each dough circle with one-quarter of the tomato sauce. Then add half the mozzarella, roasted fennel, sausage meat, pepperoni, fennel seeds and dried chilli to each one and season well.

Fold over the dough to make half-moon-shaped parcels, using the parchment paper to help you lift the dough, and crimp the edges together. With your oven still turned up as hot as it will go, cook each calzone for 10 minutes on a pizza stone or a baking sheet, then serve with the remaining sauce poured on top and fennel fronds to garnish.

PREPARATION TIME
25 minutes, plus cooling
and marinating overnight

COOKING TIME 1 hour

MARINATED MACKEREL, BABY BEETS & HORSERADISH CRÈME FRAÎCHE

My mum is half Polish and she loves a rollmop. Because of this, naturally, so do I! I tested this recipe with herrings first and it works really well but there is something about the firm flesh and oiliness of mackerel that takes so well to pickling. So here I have pickled mackerel with horseradish and beets. These flavours are all very classic but I've made a bit more of the marinade by adding in some dried chillies and lemon juice.

350ml white wine vinegar
70ml water
1 bay leaf
the rind, cut into strips,
    and juice of 1 lemon
1 teaspoon black peppercorns
½ teaspoon dried chilli flakes
    or 3–4 small dried chillies
½ teaspoon allspice berries
50g sugar
30g fine salt
1 onion, thinly sliced into
    rings
1 carrot, thinly sliced
4 mackerel, filleted (I like
    the tails left on)
a bunch of watercress,
    to garnish

For the beet salad

150g baby candy-stripe beetroot
150g baby golden beetroot
150g baby purple beetroot
3 tablespoons lemon juice
3 tablespoons olive oil
sea salt flakes and freshly
    ground black pepper

*For the horseradish crème
    fraîche*

2 tablespoons horseradish
    (freshly grated or sauce)
5 tablespoons crème fraîche
1 tablespoon lemon juice

To make the marinade, place the vinegar, water, bay leaf, lemon rind, lemon juice, peppercorns, chillies, allspice berries, sugar and salt in a small pan and heat slowly until everything melts together. Bring to the boil and then turn off the heat. Add the onion and carrot and then leave to cool.

Lay the mackerel fillets in a dish and pour over the marinade, making sure the fillets are completely immersed. Cover with cling film and leave in the fridge to marinate overnight.

Preheat the oven to 190°C/Gas Mark 5. Wrap each colour of beetroot individually in foil with a splash of water and some salt and roast for 1 hour, or until just tender. Once cooked, allow to cool in the foil and then peel and trim the beetroot. I like a little bit of the 'hair' left on them. Mix together the lemon juice and oil with plenty of seasoning in a small bowl. Place each colour of beetroot in separate bowls and dress each bowl of beetroot with one-third of the dressing. Leave to marinate for 1 hour. Just before serving you can mix the beets together.

In a small bowl, mix together the horseradish, crème fraîche and lemon juice and add plenty of seasoning.

To serve, add a blob of the horseradish crème fraîche on the side of each plate, lay 2 pieces of mackerel alongside, place the beet salad on top of the horseradish crème fraîche and garnish with some watercress.

SPICE

....

CHILLIES & WARMTH

SERVES 2
....

PREPARATION TIME
20 minutes, plus marinating

COOKING TIME
50 minutes

HARISSA PRAWNS WITH CAULIFLOWER COUSCOUS & ROASTED VEGETABLES

8–10 big fat raw king prawns,
   peeled, deveined and slit
   deeply down the backs with
   the tails left on
½ teaspoon sea salt flakes
2 tablespoons olive oil
½ teaspoon ground cumin
½ teaspoon ground coriander
1 tablespoon harissa
3 garlic cloves, finely chopped
juice of 1 lemon

For the cauliflower couscous &
roasted vegetables

1 small orange-fleshed pumpkin
   (such as Munchkin, Golden
   Nugget or onion squash),
   halved, deseeded and cut into
   8 wedges with the skin on
1 courgette, halved and then
   cut into 6 pieces
1 red pepper
3 tablespoons olive oil
250g cauliflower, trimmed and
   then cut into pieces
100ml fresh White Chicken Stock
   (see page 212)
1 tablespoon lemon juice
a small packet (about 30g) of
   coriander, roughly chopped
a small packet (about 30g) of
   flat leaf parsley, roughly
   chopped
½ small packet (about 15g) of
   mint, leaves picked and
   roughly chopped
2 tablespoons mixed seeds,
   toasted
1 tablespoon pine nuts, toasted
sea salt flakes and freshly
   ground black pepper

To serve

150g natural yogurt
1 tablespoon rose harissa

Cauliflower rice resembles couscous more than it does rice, so I had to try it out in that guise. The thing that wrecks my head about this whole thing is that cauliflower is a great vehicle for flavour in much the same way as many starchier carbohydrates. Cauliflower couscous slurps up flavours and is almost more filling than the real deal. Here I've served it with marinated harissa prawns that are quickly cooked. Damn straight, this is delicious.

....

Place the prawns in a non-reactive bowl with the salt, oil, cumin, coriander, harissa and garlic. Cover with cling film and leave to marinate in the fridge for between 30–60 minutes while you get on with the rest of the recipe.

Heat the oven to 200°C/Gas Mark 6. Place the pumpkin, courgette and whole red pepper in a roasting tray, rub with 1 tablespoon of the oil, and then season with tons of salt and pepper. (There's no need to add any spice to the vegetables as the harissa in the marinade is genuinely sufficient when the whole dish is put together later on.) Pop in the oven and roast for 45 minutes, turning the vegetables halfway through, until the vegetables are a little charred and cooked through. Remove from the oven and set aside.

Pop the red pepper in a plastic bag, seal the bag and leave to steam for 5 minutes. This will make the skin easier to peel away from the pepper's flesh. When the 5 minutes are up, take the pepper out of the bag, pull out the stalk, cut the pepper in half and remove the seeds. Peel away the skin and then slice each half pepper into 4 pieces.

While the vegetables are roasting, make the cauliflower couscous. Place the cauliflower in a food processor and blitz it on the pulse setting until it resembles something the size of couscous. Heat 1 tablespoon of oil in a frying pan with a lid and then throw in the cauliflower. Cook over a high heat for 1 minute to sear the outside of the cauliflower, stirring continuously to keep it moving as you do not want it to colour. Pour over the stock, add some salt and then pop the lid on.

Cook for 5 minutes, then remove the lid and cook it down until the stock has reduced into the rice.

Transfer the cauliflower couscous to a serving dish. Whisk together the lemon juice and 1 tablespoon of oil with some seasoning. Pour this dressing over the cauliflower. Add the herbs and mix well, then add the roasted vegetables, mixed seeds and pine nuts and give a really good mix. Leave to stand for 5 minutes and let the flavours homogenize while you make the yogurt sauce and cook the prawns.

To make the yogurt sauce, spoon the yogurt into a serving bowl, add the harissa and season. Swirl together and set aside.

Heat a frying pan until almost smoking. Lay the prawns on their sides around the pan and fry for 1 minute or until the cooked sides are a little charred. Flip the prawns over and cook for another minute or until the other sides are lightly charred and the prawns are pink. Give the prawns a good stir-fry around the pan, then add the lemon juice to the pan and stir the prawns quickly so they caramelize in the juice. Top the cauliflower couscous and roasted vegetables with the prawns, and serve with the yogurt sauce on the side.

WAT TAN HOR

a packet of fresh ho fun
  noodles (from the chiller
  cabinet at a Chinese
  supermarket)
3 tablespoons cooking oil
1 tablespoon dark soy sauce
1½ tablespoons light soy sauce
1 tablespoon oyster sauce
2 very thin slices of pork
  belly (or you could use
  unsmoked streaky bacon),
  chopped into 3cm slices
4 garlic cloves, minced
1 teaspoon peeled and grated
  fresh root ginger
1 small squid, cleaned and
  sliced into rings
10 raw king prawns
½ fish cake, sliced thinly,
  or 6 fish balls, halved
500ml fresh White Chicken Stock
  (see page 212)
a generous pinch of sugar
a pinch of white pepper
a small packet (about 250g)
  of choi sum or pak choi
3 tablespoons cornflour mixed
  with 3 tablespoons water
2 free-range eggs, beaten
fine salt

For the chilli & soy sauce

4 Thai red chillies, thinly
  sliced
4–8 tablespoons soy sauce

The first time that I ate this dish was at a street food stall in Borneo. I was being really nosey and I saw that all the tourists were eating nasi goreng and all the Chinese Malaysians were eating wat tan hor. It looks like a mess but it's so damn good. It's fresh ho fun noodles fried in soy and oyster sauce with seafood poached in a simple fresh chicken stock thickened with cornflour and egg. I eat this at least once a month at C&R Café in Chinatown in London. You really need to use fresh noodles, which you can buy from Chinatown or a Chinese supermarket. I've tried making this dish with rehydrated noodles and although it works (so use them if you really can't source fresh ones), it's not quite the same. I turned to my food writer friend Lizzie Mabbott (who blogs under the name of Hollow Legs) for help with this recipe because there are so many ways you can do it. She helped me to understand that you poach the seafood and that the sauce is very plain, which I couldn't quite believe, and gave me the tip to use unsmoked bacon as it's not easy to find thinly sliced pork belly. I spent so much time in Thailand when I was growing up that I always like to finish my wat tan hor with a spicy soy sauce that's made in the same way that the Thais would make nam pla (spicy fish sauce).

·············

To make the chilli and soy sauce, mix together the chillies and the soy sauce in a bowl and set aside.

Soak the ho fun noodles in a bowl of hot water with a good pinch of salt and separate the noodle strands carefully with chopsticks or your fingers. Drain the noodles and rinse under cold running water, then plunge the noodles into a bowl of ice-cold water so they don't stick together. When ready to use, drain the noodles and then pat them dry just before using.

Heat a wok with 1 tablespoon of oil and fry the noodles with both the soy and oyster sauces until the noodles are covered with the sauces and start to get some caramelization. Divide the noodles between 4 serving plates or, more preferably, those pasta plates with high sides.

Wipe out the wok with kitchen paper, then add 1 tablespoon

of cooking oil and fry the pork for 1–2 minutes over a high heat until the fat starts to render away and the pork gets a golden colour. Add the garlic and ginger and fry for another minute. Transfer to a bowl and set side.

Now heat up the remaining oil in the wok until fiery hot and fry the squid, prawns and fish cake or balls for few minutes. Add the fried pork and toss it around, then add the stock, sugar, white pepper and whichever greens you are using and simmer for 2–3 minutes, or until the fish is poached. Whisk in the cornflour mixture until the sauce has thickened to a gravy-like consistency. Turn off the heat and drizzle in the eggs, stirring as you go so that you get strands of egg suspended in the sauce. Pour over the noodles and serve immediately with some of the chilli and soy sauce poured over, if you like.

HOME-STYLE CABBAGE

SERVES 2

PREPARATION TIME
10 minutes

COOKING TIME
10 minutes

This was inspired by a dish from a brilliant Sichuan restaurant in Camberwell, London. It's just stir-fried cabbage but it's so blinking delicious that I could eat it for breakfast, lunch and dinner. The restaurant won't spill the details about how to make it, so I put my head together with brilliant food writers Helen Graves and Lizzie Mabbott and came up with this recipe. I like to use a normal green cabbage but actually it should be made with Chinese cabbage. I'll leave it to you to decide which type of cabbage to use.

Mix the sauce ingredients together in a small bowl and set aside.

Blanch the cabbage in a saucepan of boiling water for 30 seconds if using green cabbage or 10 seconds if using Chinese cabbage. Drain and quickly plunge into a bowl of iced water.

Heat 2 tablespoons of oil in a wok over a medium heat. Add the garlic, spring onions, Sichuan pepper and chillies and fry for 1 minute. Remove and set aside.

Drain the blanched cabbage. Pop the wok back on the hob, turn the heat up to the maximum and add the remaining oil. Once the wok is literally smoking hot, quickly add the blanched cabbage and stir-fry until heated through. Add the sauce and return the fried garlic, spring onions, Sichuan pepper and chillies to the wok. Mix well and cook for about 30 seconds, or until the sauce has thickened. Serve immediately. I would eat this simply with either white or brown rice for extra fibre.

500g green cabbage or Chinese (Napa) cabbage, chopped into large pieces
3 tablespoons vegetable oil
3 garlic cloves, finely chopped
2 spring onions (white and green parts), thinly sliced
½ teaspoon Sichuan peppercorns, crushed
3 dried chillies, deseeded and cut into small pieces

For the sauce

3 tablespoons Chinkiang vinegar (black rice vinegar)
2 tablespoons light soy sauce
1 tablespoon sugar
1 teaspoon salt
1 rounded teaspoon cornflour
2 tablespoons water

SERVES 4-6

·················

PREPARATION TIME
15 minutes, plus soaking
overnight

COOKING TIME 2¼ hours

PULLED CHIPOTLE CHICKEN WITH PINK PICKLED ONIONS

I wanted to make a chicken variation of chilli. It's not that I believe that red meat is bad for you but for midweek, when you're pushed for time and on an 'eating lighter' vibe, chicken cooks more quickly and is lower in calories. I've chopped up a whole chicken for this recipe – I honestly feel that it's better value, better for the environment and weirdly therapeutic. It's possibly the most fun kitchen skill, but if you don't want to do this then just buy chicken pieces on the bone. I've also used dried and cooked adzuki beans, which remind me of mini red kidney beans, but a good cheat would be to use a 400g can of adzuki beans or actual red kidney beans. Adzuki beans are full of dietary fibre and disease-fighting flavonoids. So on with the recipe. Chipotle chillies (dried and smoked jalapeños that have a deep spicy and smoky flavour) are essential and now available in most supermarkets and online. This recipe shows that healthy eating can be as good as, if not better than, being indulgent – and this dish is so good that it could even be cooked for entertaining.

···

200g dried adzuki beans
2 tablespoons olive oil
1 medium, whole, free-range
  chicken, jointed
2 onions, thinly sliced
1 bulb of garlic, cut in half
  horizontally
2-3 dried chipotle chillies,
  rehydrated for 10 minutes
  in 50ml boiling water
2 bay leaves
1 cinnamon stick
4 cloves
1 tablespoon ground cumin
1 tablespoon ground coriander
2 teaspoons smoked paprika
500g chopped fresh tomatoes
500ml fresh White Chicken Stock
  (see page 212)
sea salt flakes and freshly
  ground black pepper

To serve

Cauliflower Rice (see page 214)
Pink Pickled Onions (see page 131)
½ avocado, peeled, stoned and
  chopped and dressed with a
  squeeze of lime juice and a
  sprinkling of salt
100g mixed sprouting beans and
  pulses, dressed with a little
  of the Pink Pickled Onion
  juice

Place the adzuki beans in a bowl, cover with a good few inches of cold water and leave to soak forbetween 4–12 hours or overnight if you can, then boil in fresh water for 1 hour.

Heat the oil over a high heat in a large saucepan. Season the chicken pieces and then brown them in batches. It's important that you get really good colour on the chicken pieces and render down the fat as this is where the base flavour of the stew will come from. Once the chicken is browned, set it aside on a plate.

Lower the heat, add the onions to the same pan and fry them very slowly for 10–15 minutes, making sure to scrape up all the chicken residue at the bottom of the pan with a wooden spoon, until the onions have really softened, sweetened and turned a bit golden. While frying the onions, push them to one side of the pan and make space for the garlic bulb halves. Fry the garlic until the cut sides gets a bit of colour, then remove the garlic and set aside with the chicken.

≫

«   Once the onions are ready, increase the heat, add in all the spices and fry them off for a further 2 minutes. Next, add in the chopped tomatoes and give a good stir. Pop a lid on the pan and cook for 2 minutes, or until the steam has started to break the tomatoes up. Now you can remove the lid and turn the heat back down – cook for a further 10 minutes. The idea is to reduce the tomatoes until they are a really rich and thick tomato sauce.

Pour in the stock, stir and then return the chicken pieces and garlic bulb halves back to the pan and add the bay leaves. Cover with a lid and cook for 30 minutes. Drain the adzuki beans, add them to the pan and cook for another 20 minutes. Remove the chicken from the pan and set aside while you reduce the sauce. Cook the sauce until the flavour is rich and strong and the sauce has thickened.

Meanwhile, use two forks to shred the chicken, removing all the bones as you go. When the sauce is ready, return the chicken to the pan, season and stir well.

Serve the pulled chipotle chicken with the Cauliflower Rice, Pink Pickled Onions, avocado and a sprouted bean and pulse salad.

SERVES 4
....

PREPARATION TIME
20 minutes

COOKING TIME
25 minutes

MACKEREL FILLETS WITH CURRIED POTATO SALAD, SOFT-BOILED EGGS & HERBS

Okay, so this is not potato salad as we know it. It makes a terrific supper as it is but is equally great for a picnic or take-into-work lunch dish if you let everything cool, swap grilled mackerel for smoked mackerel and boil your eggs for an extra minute. Either way, it's a stonker of a way to eat potatoes and fish!

....

olive oil
1 tablespoon cumin seeds
1 tablespoon curry powder
800g Anya (or other salad) potatoes, cut into 1.5cm slices
350ml fresh White Chicken or Fish Stock (see pages 212-13, water is also fine but you'll have less flavour)
2 free-range eggs (I always go for Cotswold Legbar or Burford Brown eggs as they have bright-coloured yolks)
a small packet (about 30g) of coriander, leaves picked
a small packet (about 30g) of mint, leaves picked
½ packet (about 15g) of dill, leaves picked
2 tablespoons chives, cut into 2cm long pieces
1 tablespoon lemon juice
4 largish mackerel fillets
sea salt flakes and freshly ground black pepper

Heat 1 tablespoon of oil in a medium saucepan with a lid. Add the cumin seeds and gently toast for 1 minute or until aromatic. Add the curry powder and toast for a further 30 seconds. Tip in the potatoes, add a good pinch of salt and stir to coat thoroughly with the spices. Pour over the stock, then cover and cook the potatoes slowly over a low heat for 15 minutes, giving them a stir every now and then. The potatoes shouldn't break up because you're using a waxy salad variety but if they do, fear not, it just means that they will absorb the dressing even better. When the potatoes are cooked, remove from the heat, drain and leave them to steam in the pan with the lid on for a further 5 minutes (this makes sure they're all evenly cooked throughout). Transfer the potatoes to a mixing bowl and leave to cool a little.

Meanwhile, add the eggs to a saucepan of salted boiling water and cook for 6 minutes. Drain and then place under cold running water until the eggs are cool enough to handle. Peel the eggs: they should be soft but holding their shape well. Dry with kitchen paper and set aside.

To make the herby salad, place all the picked leaves and the chives in a bowl, then add 2 tablespoons of oil, the lemon juice and plenty of seasoning. Next, pour this over the warm (not hot) curried potatoes and stir well.

Finally, heat a little oil in a frying pan. Season the mackerel fillets with salt and pepper, then place them in the frying pan, skin-side down, and pan-fry over a fierce heat for 2–3 minutes, or until the skin is crisp and golden. Flip over the fish fillets and cook for a further minute.

Cut the boiled eggs in half. Divide the curried potato salad between 4 plates, top the salad with a mackerel fillet and half a boiled egg. Crème fraîche or soured cream would also be a nice addition.

THAI CHICKEN FRIED RICE

SERVES 4
....

PREPARATION TIME
15 minutes

COOKING TIME
10 minutes

This is a dish from my youth. When my sisters and I first started going to Thailand we would eat this on the beach pretty much every day. I returned to Thailand recently after a good 15 years and this dish is still served pretty much everywhere. I remember it always having the egg scrambled into it, but more recently it seems to be served like nasi goreng, the Malaysian version of this dish, with a fried egg on top. Thai chicken fried rice is one of my top ten things to eat and cook and it's really quick and easy to make.

....

Bash the garlic and chillies in a mortar with a pestle until all the oils burst out of them. This really is better than blitzing them together in a food processor or simply chopping them up but if you're pushed for time or don't have the equipment then you can, by all means, do either of these instead.

Heat the oil in a large wok. Add the eggs and scramble them really quickly, then scoop out of the pan and set aside on a plate. Next, add the chillies and garlic and fry for about 20 seconds, or until it becomes aromatic. Add the chicken and leave it for 1 minute (instead of stir-frying) to get some colour. Flip the chicken over and cook for another minute on the other side. Add the beans and stir-fry for 2 minutes, or until the chicken is cooked through and the beans are tender. Add the rice and stir-fry for 3–4 minutes over a really high heat – you want the rice to start to catch a bit on the base of the pan. A minute before the end of cooking time, when you're sure the rice is heated through, add the tomatoes, basil, oyster and fish sauces and sugar and cook until combined.

Meanwhile, make the nam pla. Mix together the fish sauce with the chillies and leave to macerate for 1 minute.

Serve the rice with the chopped cucumber, lime wedges and some nam pla.

4 garlic cloves, peeled
2 red Thai bird's eye chillies, chopped
2 tablespoons vegetable oil
2 free-range eggs, beaten
3cm piece of fresh root ginger, grated
2 skinless, boneless, free-range chicken breasts, chopped into large bite-sized chunks
150g long beans or French beans, cut into 3cm pieces
400g Thai Jasmine rice (or basmati rice), cooked and chilled
15 cherry tomatoes, halved
a good handful of Thai basil, plus extra to garnish
2 tablespoons oyster sauce
1 tablespoon Thai fish sauce
2 teaspoons sugar
½ cucumber, peeled and deseeded and chopped diagonally
lime wedges, to serve

For the nam pla

3 tablespoons fish sauce
4 Thai red chillies, thinly sliced

SERVES 4
....

PREPARATION TIME
30 minutes

COOKING TIME
50 minutes

GREEN MOLE IN TORTILLA BASKETS WITH RICE, BEANS & MEXICAN SALAD

I was introduced to green mole while I was in LA to learn about Mexican food and its ingredients. Green mole is thickened with seeds and flavoured with herbs, chillies and green peppers. It's lighter and way more delicious than its more famous brother that's famously finished with chocolate. The tortilla baskets are a bit of fun. Make them if you can be bothered, but the dish is just as delicious served over plain, boiled rice.

....

2 onions, 1 quartered and
   1 finely chopped
6 garlic cloves, 2 left whole
   and 4 finely chopped
5 black peppercorns
10 cloves
1 cinnamon stick
1 whole, medium, free-range
   chicken, cut into pieces,
   skin removed
1 tablespoon olive oil
100g pumpkin seeds, ground to
   dust in a food processor
1 green pepper (a poblano if
   you can find one), cored,
   deseeded and chopped
2 green chillies, chopped
a handful of coriander leaves
2 tarragon sprigs
2 flat leaf parsley sprigs
80g baby leaf spinach
400g fresh green tomatoes or
   1 x 400g can tomatillos (from
   the Mexican section of a
   supermarket)
sea salt flakes and freshly
   ground black pepper

For the tortilla baskets

4 good-quality, large corn
   tortillas
olive oil in a spray

To serve

200g basmati rice, cooked
1 x 400g can black beans,
   drained
1 avocado, peeled, stoned,
   chopped and dressed with some
   lemon or lime juice
1 Little Gem lettuce, shredded
coriander leaves

Pop the quartered onion, whole garlic cloves, whole spices and chicken pieces into a saucepan and cover with cold water. Bring to the boil, then reduce to a simmer and cook for 25 minutes, or until the chicken pieces are cooked through and tender. Strain the chicken, reserving the stock and discarding the vegetables and spices. Use 2 forks to shred the chicken pieces and set aside.

Heat the oil in a large frying pan over a high heat. Add the chopped onion, then lower the heat and fry for 10 minutes until softened and lightly golden, adding the chopped garlic for the final minute. Add the pumpkin seeds, green pepper and green chillies and fry for another minute, then add the coriander, tarragon, parsley, spinach, tomatoes or tomatillos and 300ml of the reserved chicken stock and cook the sauce for about 30 minutes, until the tomatoes have completely broken up and the sauce has reduced.

Transfer the sauce to a blender and blitz until smooth. Pass the sauce through a sieve into a clean pan and add the shredded chicken. Bring to the boil and season to taste. The green mole stew should be a little thicker than a Thai curry.

Meanwhile, make the tortilla baskets. Preheat the oven to 200°C/Gas Mark 6. Spritz the corn tortillas on both sides with the olive oil spray, then tuck them into 4 small to medium tapas dishes. Bake the tortillas for 8 minutes, or until crisped up. If you don't have 4 tapas dishes you can do this in batches as the baskets don't have to be served hot. To serve, split the rice between each tortilla basket, then top with some green mole stew, some black beans, avocado, shredded lettuce and coriander leaves.

182   SPICE / CHILLIES & WARMTH

SERVES 6-8
....

PREPARATION TIME
25 minutes

COOKING TIME
1½ hours

GREEN CHILE WITH GREEN APPLE SALSA

2 green peppers
3 tablespoons olive oil
800g minced pork (if you buy
   from a butcher ask for a
   single coarse grind)
2 onions, roughly chopped
3 garlic cloves, finely sliced
4 hot green chillies, roughly
   chopped
2 tablespoons cumin seeds
2 teaspoons ground coriander
6-8 large tomatillos or green
   tomatoes, roughly chopped or
   2 x 350g cans tomatillos
400ml fresh White Chicken Stock
   (see page 212)
½ large bunch each of parsley,
   coriander and oregano, leaves
   picked (save a few leaves for
   the garnish)
juice of 1 lime
sea salt flakes and freshly
   ground black pepper

To serve

4 flour tortillas, warmed
150ml soured cream
1 Little Gem lettuce, shredded
Green Apple Salsa (see right)

You really need to use tomatillos (Mexican Cape gooseberries) for this chile verde but in their absence tomatoes are fine.

Blacken and blister the pepper skin over a direct flame on the hob or under the grill. Pop them in a plastic food bag for 10 minutes while still hot as this will make the skins easier to peel. Peel the skins off the peppers, then halve and deseed. Roughly chop the flesh and set aside.

Heat 2 tablespoons of olive oil in a large saucepan over a medium heat. Add the pork mince in batches and a good pinch of salt and pepper. Cook for a good few minutes until browned, stirring occasionally. It's really important to get a good amount of colour on the meat for a strong meaty flavour. Remove the meat with a slotted spoon and transfer to a bowl.

In the same pan add the remaining oil, then add the onions and fry for 10-15 minutes over a medium heat until soft – for the last 2 minutes add in the garlic and chillies. Add in the cumin seeds and fry for 1-2 minutes, then add the ground coriander. Return the meat to the pan and continue cooking for another 5 minutes. Stir in the tomatillos or green tomatoes and the peppers and then pour over the stock. Reduce the heat to low and leave to bubble for about 1 hour.

Before serving, whizz all the herbs together in a blender with a pinch of salt and a splash of water until you have a green paste. Squeeze in the lime, then stir this into the meat. Scatter over the remaining herbs and serve with warm tortillas, soured cream, shredded lettuce and Green Apple Salsa.

GREEN APPLE SALSA

1 Granny Smith apple, finely
   chopped
a handful of coriander,
   roughly chopped
2 spring onions, very finely
   chopped
¼ teaspoon finely chopped
   green chilli
juice of 1 lime

Simply combine all the ingredients in a small bowl and season to taste. Leave to macerate for about 30 minutes before serving to get all the flavours in harmony.

SERVES 4
....

PREPARATION TIME
20 minutes

COOKING TIME
1½ hours

DHAL WITH SPICED CHANTENAY CARROTS, TOFU & CASHEWS

800g heritage (multicoloured)
  chantenay carrots, peeled
1 tablespoon coconut oil
1 teaspoon cumin seeds
½ teaspoon chilli flakes
4 x 1.5cm slices of firm tofu

Dhal base

1 tablespoon black mustard
  seeds
1 tablespoon cumin seeds
1 tablespoon coriander seeds
1 tablespoon white sesame seeds
¼ teaspoon dried chilli flakes
2 teaspoons vegetable oil
2 onions, chopped
6 garlic cloves, grated
a thumb-sized piece of fresh
  turmeric, grated, or
  1 tablespoon ground turmeric
a thumb-sized piece of fresh
  root ginger, grated
1 red chilli, finely chopped
100g red lentils
500ml fresh White Chicken or
  Veggie Stock (see pages
  212–13)
1 x 400ml can coconut milk
sea salt flakes and freshly
  ground black pepper

To serve

a handful of fresh coriander
  leaves
100g cashew nuts
Cauliflower Rice (see page 214)

When I'm a misery, a warming bowl of dhal is the thing that will cheer me up. I make dhal a lot, mostly because it's a storecupboard dish and I've always got the base ingredients to hand. The base of this dhal is pretty classic although it may seem weird having to blend sesame seeds with spices – they act as flavour, but also as an enricher for a really creamy finish. Then we roast a whole bunch of multicoloured heritage carrots, some tofu and cashew nuts and serve them on top for a more complete dinner. I serve this with cauliflower rice for an even bigger nutritional punch.

To make the dhal, bash the mustard seeds, cumin seeds, coriander seeds, sesame seeds and chilli flakes together with a pestle in a mortar, or use a spice grinder. Heat 1 teaspoon of oil over a low heat in a large saucepan. Add the onions and fry very slowly for about 20 minutes, or until they have really softened and start to turn golden brown. Add the garlic, turmeric, ginger and chilli and fry for 2 minutes, then add the spices and fry for 1 minute. Add the lentils to the pan and stir to coat them in the spices. Cover with the stock and coconut milk and bring to the boil, then lower the heat and simmer for 30 minutes. Season with plenty of salt and black pepper.

Preheat the oven to 200°C/Gas Mark 6. Put the carrots in a baking dish. Mix the coconut oil together with the cumin seeds, chilli flakes and plenty of salt and pepper, then rub over the carrots. Roast for 30–35 minutes, stirring halfway through. For the last 15 minutes of roasting, put the tofu and the cashew nuts into the dish with the carrots and swiftly coat in the spices. Place back in the oven, turning the tofu after 10 minutes.

Serve the dhal in bowls, each topped with tofu, roasted carrots, some cashews and fresh coriander, alongside Cauliflower Rice.

SWEET

....

DELICIOUS TREATS

PREPARATION TIME
20 minutes, plus chilling

COOKING TIME
50 minutes

BLACK VELVET CAKE

I remember first trying Nigella Lawson's chocolate Guinness cake like it was yesterday. I was testing it for a magazine feature over 10 years ago, and it blew my mind — by far the best chocolate cake I had ever made or eaten, and it wasn't slathered in chocolate icing. The contrast of dense, sticky, chocolaty and mildly boozy sponge with sharp and creamy cream cheese frosting was an instant win. So much so that when I started my website I did a homage to Nigella's cake, but added real chocolate (Nigella only uses cocoa powder) and switched the Guinness to chocolate stout. Now, here's when it gets a bit weird. My best friend Zoe and I tend to drink in hotel rooms and sing Karaoke off YouTube; by tradition, we start with 'Black Velvet' by Alannah Myles. This got me thinking: I wear black velvet A LOT, I love the song A LOT, I love the drink A LOT, I like red velvet cake A LOT; is it possible to merge all these things into one? Well, I damn well gave it a good go, and I give you my black velvet cake — the best cake you will EVER MAKE — dedicated to my Wifey. It's indulgent reducing a bottle of champagne down to syrup, so feel free to use Cava or prosecco.

··

250g unsalted butter, chopped into cubes, plus extra for greasing
250ml chocolate stout or Guinness
100g plain chocolate (70% cocoa solids), broken into pieces
35g cocoa powder
400g golden caster sugar
2 eggs
142g natural yogurt
1 tablespoon vanilla extract
275g plain flour
2½ tablespoons bicarbonate of soda

For the icing

1 x 75cl bottle of champagne
500g cream cheese
200g icing sugar
250ml double cream

Preheat the oven to 180°C/Gas Mark 4. Butter and line the base and sides of a 24cm diameter, deep, round, loose-bottomed tin.

Melt the butter together with the Guinness in a large saucepan, then add the chocolate. Once the chocolate has melted, add the cocoa powder and sugar and mix well.

In a separate bowl, whisk together the eggs, yogurt and vanilla extract, then add to the chocolate mixture. Whisk in the flour and bicarbonate of soda and whisk well until you have a smooth batter. Pour this mixture into the tin and bake for 45 minutes. If a knife comes out clean, it's done. Leave to cool in the tin.

Meanwhile, to make the icing, pour the champagne into a saucepan, bring to the boil and reduce it down until you only have 2 tablespoons left. Leave to cool completely before adding it into the cream cheese.

In a large bowl, lightly whip the cream cheese together with the icing sugar and champagne reduction until smooth.

In a separate bowl, whip the cream until it thickens but still retains its shape. Fold the cream into the cream cheese mixture until it is smooth and a spreadable consistency. I like to chill it for an hour or two while the cake is cooking and cooling.

Remove the cake from the tin. If the top is still a little crusty and domed, level it with a knife (save these bits for decoration), then cut the cake horizontally into 3 even slices. Lay the base slice on to a cake plate or stand. Spread over about 4-5 tablespoons of the icing, sandwich the next layer on and then repeat with another 4-5 tablespoons of icing and place the final layer on top. Take half the remaining icing and ice the sides of the cake, levelling it out to be smooth (the layer should be about 3mm thick). Pour the remaining icing on top and level it out flat. I make black crumbs by blitzing the excess cake in a food processor and sprinkle them neatly around the edge of the cake.

PREPARATION TIME
20 minutes, plus cooling

COOKING TIME
1¼ hours

COCONUT, BANANA & PINEAPPLE CAKE

This is a totally tropical cake, but (due to its snowball appearance) makes a wicked alternative to a Christmas cake.

··

Heat the oven to 170°C/Gas Mark 3½ and lightly grease a 20cm diameter springform cake tin.

Using a blender, blitz together the bananas and coconut milk to make a smooth paste and set aside. Using a freestanding mixer, beat together the oil and sugar (alternatively place them in a large bowl and use an electric hand whisk). Add the eggs, one at a time, beating after each addition. Beat this for a good 5 minutes, or until it's really light, pale and fluffy. Stir in the vanilla extract and banana and coconut milk mixture.

Whisk together the flour, bicarbonate of soda and salt in another bowl, fold the dry ingredients into the wet ingredients until just combined, then stir in 120g of desiccated coconut. Pour the batter into the prepared cake tin.

Bake for 1–1¼ hours, or until a metal skewer inserted in the centre of the cake comes out clean. Leave to cool in the tin. If you think the cake has a thick crust on the top, lay a warm, damp, wrung-out clean tea towel over the top of the cake while it cools and this will soften it.

To make the frosting, beat the cream cheese with the icing sugar. In a separate bowl, whip together the cream and vanilla until thickened. Now beat the cream cheese into the cream until combined. Leave in the fridge to chill while the cake is cooling.

Remove the cake from the tin. If the top is still a little crusty and domed, level it with a knife, and then cut the cake horizontally into 3 even layers. Lay the base slice on to a cake plate or stand. Spread over half the pineapple jam, and then 4–5 tablespoons of the frosting. Sandwich the next layer on, repeat with the rest of the jam and another 4–5 tablespoons of frosting, and then place the final layer on top. Take half the remaining frosting and ice the sides of the cake (the layer should be about 3mm thick). Pour the remaining icing on top and level it out flat. Cover the top of the cake with the toasted desiccated coconut and you're good to go...

3 medium overripe bananas,
   mashed
250g coconut milk
120ml vegetable oil
120g granulated sugar
2 free-range eggs
1 teaspoon vanilla extract
350g self-raising flour
½ teaspoon bicarbonate of soda
½ teaspoon fine salt
170g sweetened desiccated
   coconut, 50g toasted and
   set aside for the topping
100g Pineapple Jam
   (see page 219)

For the frosting

400g cream cheese
200g icing sugar
200ml double cream
seeds of 1 vanilla pod or
   1 teaspoon vanilla extract
   or vanilla paste

··

WHITE CHOCOLATE & CHERRY CLAFOUTIS

I still struggle with how to explain what a clafoutis is. It's a French dessert that's somewhere between a Yorkshire pudding and a custard, and it's sweet and filled with fruit: yeah, that'll do. This one is gluten-free and very custardy. It needs to be a little undercooked, especially as we're going down the chocolate route here. White chocolate and cherry is as good a combination as fish and chips or mac and cheese. To get the best out of this dish, don't let the cherries cook to gunge or the chocolate cook until it's too firm.

Chop the chocolate into chunks and place in a heatproof bowl. Melt the chocolate either over a bain-marie or in the microwave. Set aside to cool a little so that it's not boiling hot.

Now you need to make the batter. Mix together the cornflour, sugar and eggs. Slowly whisk in the milk until combined, then add the cream, vanilla extract and a pinch of salt. You should now have a thinish batter. Thoroughly beat in the melted chocolate. Now, in the same way that you would let any other batter rest, place the mixture in the fridge for 15 minutes.

Heat the oven to 190°C/Gas Mark 5. Butter a 28cm round ovenproof dish, then sprinkle with sugar. Fill the dish with the cherries and then pour over the batter. Bake for 30–35 minutes, or until well risen and golden on top but still with a gentle wobble in the middle. Leave the clafoutis to cool until warm or room temperature – it will firm up a little as it cools. Scoop out of the dish and serve.

100g white chocolate (I like the stuff with vanilla seeds in it)
2 tablespoons cornflour
20g caster sugar, plus extra for sprinkling
6 large free-range eggs
150ml milk
250ml double cream
1 tablespoon vanilla extract
pinch of fine salt
butter, for greasing
500g black cherries, pitted

SERVES 4
....

PREPARATION TIME
15 minutes

COOKING TIME
40 minutes

WAFFLES WITH BANANAS FOSTER, PINEAPPLE JAM & CHILLI & HONEY BUTTER

This is a recipe of epic proportions. There's a lot to do but it's so worth it. My friend Sami inspired this recipe. He lives in LA and is as food-obsessed as me. He couldn't wait to tell me about a waffle dish with bananas Foster and pineapple jam that he had tried while he was away. Not only did it sound delicious but it so resembled Sami, who is the sunniest, happiest creature I know. You can serve this without the ice cream for an epic brunch, but I prefer it with the ice cream and to have it for pudding.

First, make the bananas Foster. Melt the butter and sugar in a medium saucepan and then fry the bananas, cut-side down, until golden. (Leave the skin on the bananas while frying; this is to keep the bananas in shape.) Remove the bananas from the pan and set aside, cut-side up. This will encourage a crisper caramel on the face of the bananas. Pour the rum into the pan and quickly whisk, then add the double cream and spices and cook until you have a silky pouring sauce. Keep warm.

To make the chilli and honey butter melt together the butter, honey and chilli powder in a small saucepan. Keep warm.

Now cook your waffles if you haven't already (see method on page 218) and serve the hot waffles straightaway, one per person, slathered in melted chilli and honey butter, together with a spoonful of the Pineapple Jam, 2 halves of banana, a couple of spoonfuls of the rum sauce and a scoop of vanilla ice cream.

For the bananas Foster

50g butter
80g light muscovado sugar
4 bananas (unpeeled), halved
   lengthways
40ml dark rum
200ml double cream
pinch of allspice
a good grating of nutmeg

For the chilli & honey butter

80g butter
1 tablespoon runny honey
½ teaspoon hot chilli powder

To serve

4 Vanilla Waffles (see page 218)
4 tablespoons Pineapple Jam
   (see page 219)
4 large scoops vanilla
   ice cream

PREPARATION TIME
10 minutes

COOKING TIME
45 minutes

BAKED ROSÉ APRICOTS
WITH SPELT PANCAKES & PISTACHIOS

I was introduced to spelt by the old boss of Mulberry, Roger Saul, who sold up and went to live in Somerset and set up a spelt farm. Spelt flour tastes like a lighter whole-wheat flour and is BRILLIANT for baking. These spelt pancakes are terrific with roasted apricots that are baked with a spot of wine and served with a syrup. Serve with yogurt if you're being good or mascarpone if you're feeling decadent.

••

Preheat the oven to 190°C/Gas Mark 5. Place the apricot halves in an ovenproof dish, pour over the wine and sprinkle with sugar. Split the vanilla pod in half lengthways, scrape out the seeds and add both the seeds and the pod to the dish with the apricots. Add the bay leaves and cinnamon stick and mix together. Cover with foil and bake for 20 minutes. Remove the foil, gently mix, then re-cover and pop back in the oven for a further 10 minutes. Remove from the oven and let the apricots steam under the foil for 10 minutes, then remove the foil and leave to cool slightly.

Pour out the liquid from the apricots into a small saucepan or frying pan and reduce the liquid over a medium-high heat until syrupy, like a light maple syrup.

To make the spelt pancakes, combine the milk and vinegar or lemon juice in a bowl. Set aside to sit and 'sour' while you prepare the other ingredients. In a large bowl, combine the spelt flour, sugar, salt, baking powder and bicarbonate of soda. Add the beaten egg and oil or melted butter to the soured milk, stir well to combine, then pour into the bowl with the dry ingredients. Stir gently until just combined: the mixture will be lumpy.

Heat a heavy-based frying pan over a medium-high heat. Brush the pan with a little olive oil or butter. Pour a ladleful of the batter into the pan (about 60ml of batter for each pancake – I often use a ¼ cup measure instead of a ladle). Cook until the bottom of the pancake is set and browned and bubbles appear on the top, then flip and cook for another 1–2 minutes. Repeat with remaining batter – it will make exactly 8 pancakes. Serve the pancakes hot with the warm apricots, a dollop of yogurt or mascarpone, the syrup poured over and topped with chopped pistachios.

10 fresh, just ripe apricots, about 550g, halved and stoned
100ml rosé wine
50g caster sugar
1 vanilla pod
2 bay leaves
1 cinnamon stick

For the spelt pancakes

170ml milk
1 tablespoon white wine vinegar or lemon juice
100g spelt flour
1 teaspoon sugar
¼ teaspoon salt
1 teaspoon baking powder
¾ teaspoon bicarbonate of soda
1 free-range egg, beaten
1 tablespoon olive oil or melted butter, plus extra for frying

To serve

3 tablespoons Greek yogurt, fat-free Greek yogurt or mascarpone cheese
3 tablespoons chopped pistachios

MAKES 1 LITRE
....

PREPARATION TIME
10 minutes, plus infusing
and freezing

COOKING TIME 15 minutes

APRICOT KERNEL &
ALMOND MILK ICE CREAM
WITH BAKED ROSÉ APRICOTS

This dessert is so beautiful and elegant; the almond milk
is infused with the scent of apricot kernels and some of
the kernels are blended into the ice cream. It was a hard
recipe to develop and my friend Alex Fubini at the Ice
Cream Union helped me to get the quantities just right.
You see, there's not much fat in almond milk, or apricot
kernels for that matter, and I wanted to try using
unrefined rapadura sugar instead of caster sugar, all of
which affect the balance of the recipe, but we got there
in the end. This ice cream is just heavenly when served
alongside Baked Rosé Apricots.

....

Place the almond milk, almond oil and kernels in a saucepan
and heat until just starting to steam – do not let the milk
boil or it will split. Leave to infuse for 2 hours – the
infused mik should have a much more rounded apricot and almond
tinge to it.

Using a slotted spoon, remove half the kernels from the
milk and discard. Pour the infused milk and remaining
kernels into a food processor and blend until smooth,
and then add the salt. Now, return the mixture to the
pan and heat again until it is steaming but not boiling.

In a large bowl, whisk together the egg yolks, sugar and
xanthan gum until fluffy. Whisk in the hot infused milk
and kernels mixture and then pour it all back into the
pan. There is now enough fat and sugar to stabilize the
mixture so place the pan over a low heat and whisk until
the mixture comes up to the boil and thickens to a rich
custard. Remove from the heat, cover the surface of the
custard with a layer of cling film and leave to cool.

Once cool, pour the custard into an ice cream machine
and churn according to the manufacturer's instructions
until it's frozen. Transfer to a 1-litre sealable plastic
container and freeze for a minimum of 5 hours. Serve
with Baked Rosé Apricots and sprinkled with crushed
Amaretti biscuits.

1 litre best-quality pressed
  almond milk (I use The
  Pressery brand)
1½ tablespoons sweet almond oil
100g apricot kernels (you can
  now buy these from health
  food shops – yippee!)
½ teaspoon salt
8 free-range egg yolks
130g rapadura sugar or 110g
  caster sugar
½ teaspoon xanthan gum
Baked Rosé Apricots, to serve
  (see page 200)
Amaretti biscuits, crushed, to
  serve

You will also need an ice cream
  machine

MAKES 10 SLICES

....

PREPARATION TIME
20 minutes, plus chilling and
cooling

COOKING TIME 1½ hours

MAPLE SYRUP, ORANGE & ROSEMARY TART

If you asked me to choose a favourite dessert it'd be hard, but if I HAD TO then one of the best has got to be treacle tart. I bloody love it, especially warm from the oven with crème fraîche. I'm a sucker for some rosemary and salt with anything sweet (it just works), so I tried to create a maple syrup version of this pud with orange as the main flavour and infused with some rosemary for good measure. And do you know what? It was a revelation! It beats treacle tart hands down. Don't believe me? Try it!

....

Heat the oven to 190°C/Gas Mark 5. Dust a kitchen work surface with flour and roll out the pastry so it's about 2mm thick. Very carefully line a deep 24cm diameter tart tin, leaving the excess pastry overhanging the edge of the tin (this will be trimmed off after the pastry's been blind-baked). Place the pastry-lined tin in the freezer for 10 minutes. Line the raw pastry case with greaseproof paper, fill it with baking beans and blind-bake for 20 minutes. Remove the baking beans and greaseproof paper and pop it back in the oven for a further 10 minutes. Remove from the oven and leave to cool. Lower the oven temperature to 140°C/Gas Mark 1. When the pastry case is cool, use a knife to carefully trim the pastry, carving off the excess against the side of the tin. Use a pastry brush to brush away any crumbs.

Put the orange and lemon rinds and juices in a saucepan with the rosemary, golden syrup, maple syrup, butter and salt. Bring to the boil and then remove from the heat and leave to cool until the mixture is warm enough to sip. This should now have a really great balance of citrus, rosemary and maple syrup flavours and will be very sweet. Remove and discard the rosemary sprigs, as we don't want those in the tart, just the flavour of rosemary infused into the dish.

In a bowl, mix together the citrus syrup with the breadcrumbs and leave to stand for 5 minutes so that the breadcrumbs absorb the syrup. Mix in the egg and egg yolk, then spoon the mixture into the pastry case and bake for 50–60 minutes until it is set but still has a bit of a wobble in the centre. Remove from the oven and leave to cool for 10 minutes before serving with crème fraîche.

plain flour, for dusting
250g ready-made, ready-rolled
  sweet shortcrust pastry (pâte
  sucrée if you can find it)
grated rind and juice of
  2 oranges
grated rind and juice of
  1 lemon
4–5 rosemary sprigs
350g golden syrup
170ml maple syrup
1 tablespoon butter
½ teaspoon sea salt flakes
110g fresh breadcrumbs
1 free-range egg plus 1 egg
  yolk, lightly beaten
crème fraîche, to serve

PREPARATION TIME
20 minutes, plus setting

COOKING TIME
25–30 minutes

MOLTEN CARAMEL & CHOCOLATE PUDDINGS

Chocolate with salted caramel is the best pudding combination ever. If it (or rhubarb) is on the menu then I have to order it – and I'm not especially a pudding person. Here is the ultimate version of this combination of ingredients: a baked chocolate pudding with a molten base of salted caramel. It's hot, it's gooey, it's salty, sweet and chocolatey, and it's messy home cooking. I don't think you've eaten this right unless it's all over your face and you're licking the dish.

....

Butter 6 medium ramekins (or a 5 x 11cm baking dish) then dust with rice flour.

To make the caramel, melt the sugar with a splash of water in a saucepan over a medium heat until it is a light golden colour. Whisk in the butter, then the double cream and finally the salt. Pour the caramel about 1cm deep into the base of prepared ramekins or dish, then leave in the fridge for 20 minutes to set. Reserve any caramel leftover for serving.

When the caramel has almost set, start making the chocolate pudding. Preheat the oven to 140°C/Gas Mark 1. Melt together the butter, chocolate, cocoa powder and salt in a heatproof bowl over a bain-marie, stirring until it is smooth. In a separate bowl, beat the eggs and sugar together until light and well creamed. Beat in the maple syrup, vanilla extract and double cream, then pour in the chocolate mixture and mix well. Pour on top of the set caramel and bake in the oven for 25–30 minutes, or until it's puffed up and set on top but still has a slight wibble in the very centre. Remove from the oven and leave to sit for 5 minutes. Serve with a dollop of crème fraîche and any leftover caramel.

150g unsalted butter, plus
  extra for greasing
1 tablespoon rice flour,
  for dusting
160g good-quality chocolate
8 tablespoons cocoa powder
small pinch of sea salt flakes
4 free-range eggs
200g caster sugar
3 tablespoons maple syrup
1 teaspoon vanilla extract
3 tablespoons double cream
crème fraîche, to serve

For the caramel

150g caster sugar
65g butter, diced
100ml double cream
1 teaspoon sea salt flakes

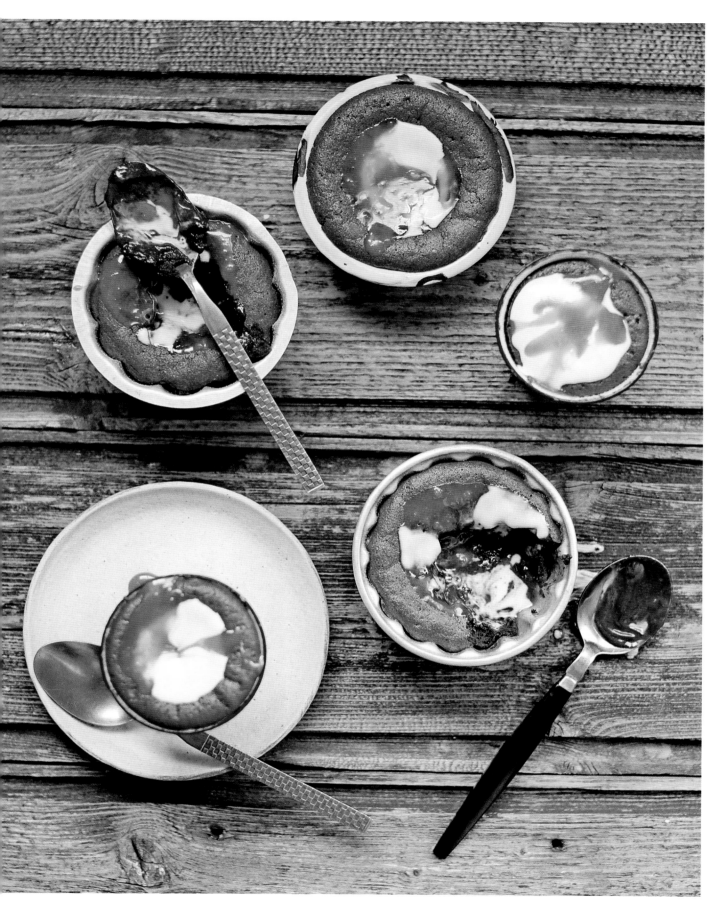

THAI STICKY RICE
WITH MANGO

I'm dedicating another recipe to one of my greatest friends
of all time, my wifey, Zoe Willis. Willis and I went to Thailand
together and spent our time eating some incredible food,
travelling round, experiencing not a single same thing –
except maybe our obsession with sticky rice and mango. It was
like our home comfort. By the time we got home, after an epic
day we would get into bed, order some sticky rice and watch a
flick. In a place of insane, sticky rice made us sane. It's
our thing. So this one's for you, Zoe...

Place the glutinous rice in a bowl, cover with cold water and
leave covered for 1 hour. You can leave it up to 5 hours, but
the rice starts to break down a bit.

Okay, so this is where it gets a bit annoying if you're
not used to it: steaming the rice. I use a bamboo steamer
and I line it with wet muslin or even strong kitchen
paper is fine. Drain and wash the rice, and then tip it
into the lined steamer. Cover with some more wet muslin
or kitchen paper and put the lid on the steamer. Place the
steamer in a lidded pan of boiling water, where the water
only just reaches up to the base of the steamer. I use a
lidded wok for this. Pop the lid on and steam the rice at
a low to medium simmer for 20 minutes. Alternatively, if
you own a proper steamer, just steam the rice in the
muslin or kitchen paper for 20 minutes according to the
steamer instructions.

Meanwhile, make a coconut caramel. Heat the coconut
milk in a small pan over a high heat, add the palm sugar
and salt and stir until dissolved. Bring to the boil for
a few seconds, then turn off the heat.

When the rice has steamed and cooked all the way
through with no crunchy bits in the middle, turn it out
into a mixing bowl. Pour over the coconut caramel and
give it a good mix. Next, cover the bowl with cling film and
leave for 30 minutes. The rice will absorb all the coconut
and it will be well seasoned. And completely sticky.

Now here's the hard part; technically, you should wait
until it's at room temperature to eat it. Sometimes I can
do this, other times not a hope. Serve with sliced mango
and sprinkled with sesame seeds.

220g Thai glutinous rice
170ml creamy coconut milk
60g palm sugar, grated or
  finely chopped
½ teaspoon sea salt flakes
1 really good ripe mango,
  peeled, stoned and sliced
toasted black and white sesame
  seeds, to serve

BASICS

MAKES 1.5 LITRES
....

PREPARATION TIME
10 minutes

COOKING TIME
3½ hours

WHITE CHICKEN STOCK
& OTHER HOMEMADE STOCK

Stock-making is a slow process but I find it really therapeutic, and I'm a massive advocate because it means you are using every last morsel of an animal. I save chicken carcasses in a bag in the freezer after I've had a roast chicken and, in fact, I also save any other leftover chicken on the bone. If you have trouble finding raw carcasses, then you can use about 800g of chicken wings instead. Fresh chicken stock is great in brothy or puréed soups, stews, gravies and wherever else it is called for. It freezes brilliantly, so invest in lots of 400ml sealable plastic containers and then you can have stock to hand whenever you need it. I've included a few other recipes using the same basic method for when you might need other flavoured stocks.

....

3 roast chicken carcasses
(after each roast meal
remember to pop the carcass
into a bag and freeze it until
you have enough saved up)
or 3–4 raw chicken carcasses
(these can be bought from
your butcher)
1 pig's trotter, cut into slices
by a butcher (optional – this
makes a really gelatinous
stock)
2 onions, quartered
1 bulb of garlic, halved
horizontally
2 carrots, chopped into
3 pieces
2 leeks, chopped into 3 pieces
a few fresh herbs, such as
parsley stalks and thyme
sprigs
1 bay leaf
8 black peppercorns

Place all the ingredients in a large, deep saucepan, cover with cold water and slowly bring to the boil. Scum will rise to the surface as the stock begins to boil so use a large spoon or a small ladle to skim off the scum and any fat. When the stock has reached boiling point, reduce the heat and gently simmer the stock for 3 hours, skimming the top as it cooks – most of the skimming will need to be done during the first 30 minutes of cooking time. (It's important to make sure the stock doesn't boil at this stage or the bubbles will knock away at the proteins and make the stock cloudy.) As the stock cooks it will begin to reduce; if the water level falls below the contents of the pot, add a little more cold water – this will reveal any scum hiding at the bottom of the pan.

When the 3 hours are up, place a fine sieve over a large pan or bowl and strain the stock to collect all the flavoursome juices. At this stage, the stock may not have much flavour so you will need to slowly reduce the liquid in order for the flavours to be condensed. To do this, pour the stock into a pan, if necessary, bring the stock to the boil, reduce the heat and simmer to slowly reduce the stock, tasting it every so often, until you have the right intensity of chickenyness. Do not season your stock. Obviously, the stock will taste better if you season it but it will still need tweaking once it's used in other dishes so its better to leave it unseasoned for now.

....

You can use the stock straightaway or let it cool and then transfer it to the fridge or freezer. A good chicken stock will have a really chickeny essence and it will turn to jelly when it is refrigerated.

Dark chicken stock: For a richer stock that's great with gravies and meat stews, roast the veggies and chicken carcasses in a really hot oven for 30 minutes, or until they have become golden and caramelized (be careful not to burn them or the charred flavour will transfer to the stock), then cook the stock as opposite.

Beef or veal stock: Swap the chicken carcasses for 2kg of beef or veal shin bones and cook in the same way as for the dark chicken stock, cooking the stock for 3-4 hours before straining. Veal stock is the best to use when making meat gravies as it will give you that flavour you normally only get in restaurants.

Fish stock: Swap the chicken carcasses for the carcasses (but not heads) of 3 largish white fish or 1kg of fish bones. Salmon or tuna make horrid stock so I would go for sea bass, halibut, haddock and so on. Cook in the same way as for the white chicken stock, but only cook the stock for 20 minutes before straining. There is a fine line when it comes to making fish stock and it can become quite rancid if cooked for too long.

Veggie stock: Leave out the chicken carcasses and double the quantity of vegetables in the white chicken stock recipe, adding 2 parsnips and some of the outer leaves of a cabbage. Place in a large saucepan, cover with cold water and cook gently for 20 minutes. As with fish stock, vegetable stock can taste and smell too strong if it's cooked for too long – think of the stewed veg you used to get at school!

PREPARATION TIME
5 minutes

COOKING TIME
10 minutes

CAULIFLOWER RICE

Everyone is going mad for spiralized vegetables and vegetable rices. I wasn't convinced about them to begin with but on whole don't knock it 'til you try it rule absolutely came into its own here. My friend Elly, who owns Pear Café in Bristol, whips up some of the most incredible low-calorie concoctions that are a 5:2 dieter's dream. It was at a pop-up that Elly organized that I first tried cauliflower rice in a salad with purple cauliflower, tahini and Sriracha chilli sauce. It was delicious. The cauliflower had lost its strong flavour and was a terrific medium for soaking up sauce! The recipe is so simple, I'm now hooked and into trying out loads of rice and couscous recipes with this method. Serve it with Pulled Chipotle Chicken (see page 175) or Dahl with Spiced Chantenay Carrots, Tofu & Cashews (see page 186).

Place the cauliflower in a food processor and blitz it on the pulse setting until it resembles something the size of rice.

Heat the oil or butter in a frying pan with a lid. Throw in the cauliflower and cook over a high heat for a minute or so to sear the outside, stirring continuously. You don't want the cauliflower to colour, so keep it moving.

Pour over the stock, add some salt and cover with the lid. Cook for 5 minutes, then remove the lid and cook until the stock has reduced into the rice. It's now ready to serve.

1 cauliflower, about 250–300g, trimmed
1 tablespoon oil or butter of your choice
50ml fresh White Chicken, Fish or Beef Stock (see pages 212–13, or water is fine)
a good pinch of sea salt flakes

SERVES 4
....

PREPARATION TIME
5 minutes

COOKING TIME
10 minutes

HOLLANDAISE SAUCE

Don't freak out at the idea of making hollandaise sauce. There are foodie scaremongers out there but it's really not that tricky to make this sauce, all you need is patience. Just let the butter trickle really, really slowly into the food processor and watch your sauce turn from slick butter into a thick, emulsified sauce. It doesn't keep very well, so it's best to make it to order. For béarnaise sauce, which is an absolute classic with steak, just add chopped tarragon and chervil to your finished hollandaise.

....

To make the reduction, place all the ingredients in a small saucepan and bring to the boil. Keep boiling to reduce the amount of liquid until you have just 2 tablespoons left. Strain the reduction into a cold bowl.

Whizz the egg yolks in a food processor with a pinch of salt and then pour in half the reduction.

With the machine running, pour the butter into the food processor very, very slowly – 1 teaspoon at a time – until half of it has been used up (the sauce should be fairly thick at this point). Pour in the remaining butter in a fine stream until it has all combined. Season the sauce with salt, lemon juice and the remaining reduction if it needs it.

Alternatively, you can make the sauce by hand, beating the ingredients together with a balloon or electric hand whisk in a heatproof bowl set over a bain-marie.

For the reduction

1 shallot, finely chopped
6 tablespoons white wine
  vinegar
3 black peppercorns
1 bay leaf
2 blades of mace

For the sauce

4 free-range egg yolks
225g hot melted butter
squeeze of lemon juice
sea salt flakes

MAKES about 300ml schmaltz
and 100g gribenes
....

PREPARATION TIME
10 minutes
COOKING TIME 40 minutes

SCHMALTZ & GRIBENES

Most people know very little about Jewish food. Many of us will have heard of, or possibly even tried, chopped liver (it's a coarse pâté) but not many people who aren't Jewish or 'au fait' with Jewish cuisine will be familiar with gribenes. They are a by-product of making schmaltz (chicken fat that is rendered down and then used to cook and flavour dishes). What you're left with after making schmaltz is little nuggets of chicken skin. These are then rendered down even more but this time with onions, until you have crisp roasted chicken skin with caramelized onions. Gribenes are the stuff that dreams are made of, and they're used to garnish numerous dishes. I use them in Chopped Liver with Egg & Gribenes (see page 65) and in the Egg & Onions sandwich (see page 89).

With scissors or a sharp knife, cut the chicken skin into 8–10mm cubes.

Heat a frying pan over a medium-low heat and add the chicken skin. Increase the heat until the skin starts to fry, then reduce the temperature until it is fairly low and cook the chicken skin very slowly for 25–30 minutes, or until the fat has rendered out of it. The chicken skin should let out about 300ml of fat. You need to fry the skin slowly over a low heat as you don't want any colour to the skin. Strain the fat from the chicken skin, reserving the fat (schmaltz) as it's as precious as gold dust.

Return the chicken skin to the pan. There is no need to wipe out the pan as you will need the excess chicken fat to help the skin crisp up. Fry the skin for 2 minutes, or until some more fat starts to come out. Then add the onion and sauté with the chicken skin until the onions break down and start to caramelize. Season with salt and continue to fry until the skin is roasted and has turned golden and the onions have caramelized. Pour any excess fat into the reserved schmaltz and drain the gribenes on kitchen paper, adding more salt if necessary, and allow to crisp up.

The schmaltz will last up to a month in the fridge but I suggest you use the gribenes on the day you make them.

500g raw chicken skin (you can buy this from a butcher or collect it whenever you skin some chicken and freeze until you have enough for this recipe)
½ onion, very thinly sliced
a good pinch of sea salt flakes

GIZZI'S KIMCHI

MY LIFE REVOLVES around kimchi. It's my lifeline. I love it so much I even called my cat Kimchi. The hot, tangy, crunchy cabbage is in my veins! It's an acquired taste and takes a bit of time to get your head round it. If I'm honest, I actually prefer it served in a Western way, rather than a Korean way, such as in cheese toasties or with cured meats. Anyway, for those who are new to it, it's a fermented cabbage, a bit like sauerkraut, but oh so very fiery! You make it a couple of weeks in advance, a bit like a pickle or chutney, and allow it to naturally ferment and go sour. It's served in Korea as an accompaniment to almost every dish. There are at least two recipes in this book that use it, so it's good to have a supply you've made yourself (although I do sometimes buy shop-bought stuff from the Asian supermarkets). It's fun to make and it's messy. Try it at least once. The longer it ferments, the tangier it gets. I like mine really tangy and fizzy, but most people like it quite light.

....

1 small to medium head of Chinese Napa cabbage
50g sea salt flakes
50g plus 2 tablespoons sugar
1 bulb of garlic, cloves separated
80g peeled fresh root ginger
50–60g kochukaru (Korean chilli powder)
40ml fish sauce
40ml usukuchi (light Korean soy sauce)
1 tablespoon jarred salted shrimp
6 spring onions (green and white parts), julienned
1 Korean pear or sharp apple, such as Granny Smith, peeled, cored and julienned

Trim the cabbage of outside leaves, and then cut the cabbage into quarters through the root.

In a saucepan heat about 300ml water, add the salt, 50g sugar and stir until dissolved. Pour into a large non-reactive container that the cabbage will fit into and cover with 4 litres of cold water. If the water is totally cool add in the cabbage and leave to brine overnight.

Blend the garlic, ginger, kochukaru, fish sauce, usukuchi, shrimp and remaining sugar in a food processor until completely puréed. If it is very thick and sludgey, add water about 50ml at a time until it becomes a custard-like consistency. Stir in the spring onions and pear or apple.

Drain the cabbage. Fully cut the cabbage through the core and into quarters and rub the marinade into every leaf. Wedge each quarter into a large 3-litre Kilner jar or the largest jar you can find, then refrigerate. The kimchi will be tasty after 24 hours, but it will be better in a week and at its prime in 2 weeks. It will still be good for another couple weeks after that, though it will grow way stronger and funkier.

VANILLA WAFFLES

This is a really simple recipe to ensure really light, fluffy waffles that have hints of vanilla. Serve them the American way, with smoked streaky bacon and real maple syrup; the Belgian way, slathered in chocolate sauce; or my way (see page 197), with chilli and honey butter, pineapple jam and bananas Foster.

Preheat a waffle iron according to the manufacturer's instructions.

Sift together the flour, baking powder, salt and sugar in a bowl. In a separate bowl, whisk together the milk, egg yolks and vanilla extract and pour it over the dry ingredients, stirring very gently until half combined. Pour in the melted butter and continue mixing until the batter is fully combined.

In a separate, spotlessly clean bowl, whisk the egg whites until stiff, and then fold them into the batter until fully combined and you have a smooth, fluffy batter.

Brush the waffle iron with a little melted butter and then pour a ladleful of the batter into the iron and cook for 6–8 minutes, or until the waffle is crisp and golden. Repeat with the rest of the mixture and set aside the cooked waffles under a clean tea towel to keep warm. Serve the waffles piping hot with whichever toppings you like.

Store any leftover batter in the fridge for up to 2 days.

250g plain flour
2 teaspoons baking powder
½ teaspoon salt
50g caster sugar
250ml milk
2 free-range egg yolks
1 tablespoon vanilla extract
110g unsalted butter, melted,
  plus extra for brushing
4 free-range egg whites

You will also need a waffle iron

PREPARATION TIME
10 minutes

COOKING TIME
55 minutes

PINEAPPLE JAM

Everyone said that you couldn't make pineapple jam. Everyone lied. You can — and it's amazing. You just need to use a pectin-boosted preserving sugar. Don't do what I always do, which is to try and eat scalding sugar off a metal spoon immediately after its cooked: that's just stupid...

....

Cut the pineapple into large chunks. Pop them in a food processor and pulse until the pineapple has broken down into 5mm pieces. It is best to use a food processor as the pineapple releases a lot of juice but if you don't have one then hand-chopping finely with a cross-chop motion is okay.

Place the pineapple in a medium saucepan, cover with the water and cook slowly for 3 minutes, or until the pineapple is soft. Add the sugar and lime or lemon juice and stir over the heat until the sugar grains have melted. Cook for another 45 minutes, or until the pineapple has become like a loose jam. It will thicken a bit on cooling, so you only need about 2 tablespoons of liquid left in the base of the pan.

Pour the jam into a sterilized jam or Kilner jar, top with a piece of waxed paper and seal tightly. Allow the jam to cool in the jar and then store in a cool, dark cupboard for up to a year. I would leave the jam to mature and develop its flavour for at least a week before eating, though it's obviously fine to eat it straightaway once cool.

1 large pineapple, skinned and
  cored (about 550g flesh)
200ml water
250g preserving sugar
50ml lime or lemon juice

INDEX

A

almond milk 10, 16, 202–3
almonds, toasted 104
amaranth flakes 85
anchovy
  in arrabiatta 156
  in Caesar salad 54, 55
  dips 36, 38
  dressing 104
  tapenade 151
apples 17, 185
apricots 198–201, 202–3
asparagus, crudités 36
avocado
  with carnitas 130
  in ceviche 46
  chipotle chicken 175
  cucumber & buttermilk soup
    18–19
  with green mole 182
  guacamole 69
  prawns & Marie Rose sauce
    90–1
  salad with wasabi, wakame &
    spring onions 44–5
  super green smoothie 17
  superfood salad 53

B

bahn cuou 29
banana 16, 194, 196–7
bean sprouts 30–1, 175
beans, adzuki 175
beans, butter 148–9
beans, edamame 53
beans, French 58–9, 180
beans, garbanzo 121–3
beans, ginkgo 24
beans, green 120
beans, pinto, refried 68–70
beans, runner 58–9
bee pollen, in smoothie 16

beef
  bolognese sauce 134–5
  featherblade bourguignon
    127–9
  Korean noodle salad 26–7
  in meatballs 139
  stock 213
beetroot
  chlodnik (soup) 20–1
  salad with mackerel 165
  Sophia's pinkalilli 58–9
berries 82, 85
bhel puri salad 42–3
black velvet cake 190–3
blender 13
blood sugar 8, 9
bo ssam, pork belly 106–7
bolognese sauce 134–5
bowls, mixing 13
bread
  egg & onion sandwich 88–9
  kimcheese Cuban sandwich
    92–3
  mozzarella en carozza 86–7
  pangrattato 156
brie, in mushroom pie 94
broccoli 53, 104–5
bulgar wheat 108, 110
burrata 104–5, 116–17
butter
  garlic 75
  hot chilli 148
  sage & lemon 112
  sesame 60–1
buttermilk 18–19, 20–1, 72

C

cabbage 174, 217
cake 190–3, 194
calzone, roasted fennel &
  pepperoni 162–4
Camembert, mushroom pie 94

caramel & chocolate pudding
  206–7
carbs 8
carnitas 93, 130–3
carrots 36, 41, 186–7
cashew nuts 102, 186
cauliflower
  with cheese sauce 98–9
  couscous with prawns &
    vegetables 168–71
  crudités 36
  grilled, with hummus &
    cashew brittle 102–3
  pickled vegetable salad 41
  rice 158–61, 175, 214
  Sophia's pinkalilli 58–9
celery, crudités 36
ceviche, with yuzu, sesame &
  kumquats 46–8
cherry & white chocolate
  clafoutis 195
chia seeds 85
chicken
  with Caesar salad 54–7
  green mole in tortilla
    baskets 182–3
  Kievs, with garlic 74–6
  Korean fried 71–3
  liver 64–5, 134
  in mulligatawny soup 22
  pho with daikon noodles 23
  & potato stew, Korean 120
  pulled chipotle, & pink
    pickled onions 175–7
  samgyetang 24–5
  satay sauce & spiralized
    vegetables 77–9
  schmaltz & gribenes 216
  Spanish stew with chorizo,
    sherry & garbanzo beans
    121–3
  stock 212–13

Thai fried rice 180–1
chickpeas 42, 121–3
chlodnik (soup) 20–1
chocolate
  black velvet cake 190–1
  & caramel pudding 206–7
  & cherry clafoutis 195
choi sum, wat tan hor 172
chopping boards 12
chorizo & chicken stew 121
chutney 42
clafoutis, white chocolate &
  cherry 195
clams (vongole) 144–5, 154–5
coconut, banana & pineapple
  cake 194
coconut milk 85, 208
cods' roe & salmon dip 37
corn on the cob 46
courgettes 58, 78, 139, 168
couscous, cauliflower 168
cream cheese icing 190, 194
croutons 54
crudités 36–9
cucumber
  avocado & buttermilk soup
    18–19
  bhel puri salad 42
  in chlodnik 20
  crudités 36
  Korean noodle salad 26–7
  Sophia's pinkalilli 58–9

D
daikon 23, 26–7, 78
dairy products 10
dak dori tang 120
dates 16, 42
dhal with spiced carrots,
  tofu & cashews 186–7
diet, 80/20 rule 8
dips 36, 37, 38, 60–1

duck, Thai roast & watermelon
  salad 49–51

E
eggs
  hardboiled 20, 26, 65, 89
  & onion sandwich 88–9
  poached 22, 148–9
  scrambled 180
  soft-boiled 54, 158, 178–9
equipment 12–13

F
fat 9
fennel
  calzone 162–4
  with fish stew 144–5
  pickled vegetable salad 41
  salad 113
fish
  cake, wat tan hor 172
  ceviche with yuzu, sesame &
    kumquats 46–8
  in stew 28–9, 144–5
  stock 213
food processor 13

G
garlic 74, 115, 148
gigantes with eggs, yogurt,
  herbs & chilli 148–9
ginseng 24
glycaemic index (GI) scale 8
goat's curd 41
goulash, ox cheek 125–6
gravy 10
green juices 10, 17
gremolata, marrowbone 95, 96
gribenes 65, 89, 216
guacamole 69

H
haloumi, with tapenade 150–1
horseradish 44, 165
hummus 102, 108, 110

I
ice cream, almond milk 202–3

K
kale
  chips 34–5
  super green smoothie 17
  superfood salad 53
kedgeree, mackerel 158–61
kimchi 24, 92–3, 106, 217
kiwifruit, in smoothie 17
knives 12
kumquats 46

L
lamb
  merguez shepherd's pie with
    cauliflower mash 140–3
  'shawarma', with pittas,
    hummus & pomegranate
    tabbouleh 108–10
lasagne 136–7
latkes, potato 66–7
lentils 22, 186–7
liver, chicken 64–5, 134

M
mackerel
  baby beets, horseradish &
    and cauliflower rice
    kedgeree 158–61
  crème fraîche 165
  with potato salad, eggs &
    herbs 178–9
mango 85, 208–9
maple syrup, orange &
  rosemary tart 204–5

INDEX

marrowbone, gremolata 95, 96
meat 10
meatballs 138–9
melon, Canteloupe 116
merguez shepherd's pie 140–3
mixers 13
monkfish, in fish stew 144–5
mozzarella en carozza 86–7
mul naengmyeon 26–7
mulligatawny soup 22
mushrooms, wild, truffle &
  Tunworth pie 94

N

nachos 68–70
n'duja, with vongole 154
noodles
  chickpea 42
  daikon 23
  ho fun 172–3
  pad Thai 30–1
  rice 29
  soba 26–7
  spiralized vegetable 77–8

O

oats, porridge 82–3, 84–5
olives 41, 151, 156
onions
  & egg sandwich 88–9
  pink pickled 131, 133, 175–7
  silver skin 58–9
ox cheek goulash 125–6

P

pad Thai 30–1
pak choi, wat tan hor 172
pancakes, spelt 200
pancetta 134
pangrattato 156
pans 12
Parma ham 116

passion fruit 85
pasta
  arrabiata with sardines &
    pangrattato 156–7
  bolognese sauce 134–5
  lasagne 136–7
  with meatballs 139
  orza with fish stew 144–5
  spätzle 126
  truffle pappardelle 152–3
  vongole with spaghetti &
    n'duja 154–5
paté, chicken liver 65
peach 85, 116–17
pears 17, 26–7, 217
pickles 40–1, 58–9, 131, 133,
  175–7
pie, mushroom, truffle &
  Tunworth 94
pineapple, grilled salsa 130
pineapple jam 219
  coconut & banana cake 194
  with waffles 197
pitta bread 108–10
pizza dough 163–4
pomegranate 42, 108, 110
ponzu 115
pork
  belly 106–7, 172
  bolognese sauce 134
  green chile 184–5
  leftover roast 93
  in meatballs 139
  pig's trotter 212
  shoulder, carnitas 130–3
porridge 82–3, 84–5
potato
  alternatives 214
  & chicken stew 120
  creamy mash 128–9
  curried salad 179
  latkes 66–7

prawns
  with avocado & Marie Rose
    sauce 90–1
  with cauliflower couscous &
    vegetables 168–71
  in fish stew 28–9, 144–5
  Korean roasted oil 90
  pad Thai 30–1
  wat tan hor 172
pumpkin, roasted 168

Q

quinoa 53, 85

R

radishes
  with avocado, wasabi &
    wakame salad 44
  crudités 36
  pickled vegetable salad 41
  superfood salad 53
rice
  cauliflower 158–61, 175, 214
  fried, Thai chicken 180–1
  with green mole 182
  Indian puffed 42
  Korean 24
  noodles 29
  saffron risotto 96, 97
  Thai sticky 208–9
  wrappers 29

S

salad
  avocado, wasabi, wakame &
    spring onion 44–5
  beetroot 165
  bhel puri 42–3
  burrata with peach, melon &
    Parma ham 116–17
  Caesar, with chicken 54–7
  curried potato 179

fennel 113
mul naengmyeon 26–7
pickled vegetable 40–1
superfood 52–3
Thai roast duck &
  watermelon 49–51
salmon, smoked 37, 52–3
salsa 68, 130, 185
salt, dipping 24
samgyetang 24–5
sandwiches 88–9, 92–3
sardines, with arrabiata &
  pangrattato 156–7
sauce
  béchamel 137
  bolognese 134
  cheese 98
  chilli & soy sauce 172
  Hollandaise 153, 215
  Korean chilli 72
  Marie Rose 90
  nam pla 180
  ponzu 115
  satay 79
  ssam jam 106
  tomato 86
sausages 121, 140–3, 154,
  162–4
scales 13
schmaltz 65, 89, 216
sea bass 46–8, 113
sea bream 28–9, 113
seaweed, wakame 44
sesame 60–1, 107, 115
shallots, crispy 22, 29, 79,
  98, 102
shepherd's pie, merguez, &
  cauliflower mash 140–3
smoothies 16–17
Sophia's pinkalilli 58–9
soups 18–29
spätzle 126

spelt pancakes 200
spiralizing 13, 23, 78, 139
spring onion 41, 44, 53, 107
squid 28–9, 144–5, 172
ssam, jam sauce 106
stew
  fish 29, 144–5
  Korean chicken & potato 120
  ox cheek goulash 125–6
  Spanish chicken 121–3
stock 10, 212–13
sugar 9
sweet potato, noodles 78

T
tabbouleh 108, 110
tamarind & date chutney 42
tapenade 151
tart, maple syrup, orange &
  rosemary 204–5
Thai-style dishes
  chicken fried rice 180–1
  pad Thai 30–1
  roast duck & watermelon
    salad 49–51
  sticky rice with mango
    208–9
'tigers' milk 46
tofu 30–1, 186–7
tomatillos 182, 185
tomatoes
  arrabiatta 156
  bhel puri salad 42
  bolognese sauce 134
  calzone with roasted fennel
    162–4
  chipotle chicken 175
  in fish stew 28–9, 144–5
  gigantes with eggs & yogurt
    148–9
  green chile 185
  in green mole 182

in guacamole 69
meatball sauce 138–9
mozzarella en carozza 86–7
salad 150–1
salsa 68
tortilla
  baskets 182–3
  with carnitas 130–3
  chips, nachos 68–70
  with green chile 185
truffle 94, 153
tuna, tataki with yuzu,
  ginger & garlic 114–15

V
veal
  bolognese sauce 134–5
  braised tail, with risotto &
    gremolata 95–7
  chops, with sage & lemon
    butter 111–12
  stock 213
vegetables
  crudités 36
  in diet 10
  pickled salad 40–1
  roasted 168–71
  spiralized noodles 77–8
  stock 213
vongole (clams) 144–5, 154–5

W
waffles, vanilla 196–7, 218
walnut bagna cauda 38
wat tan hor 172–3
wasabi dressing 44
watermelon salad with Thai
  roast duck 49–51

Y
yogurt, garlicky 148
yuzu 46

ACKNOWLEDGEMENTS

An Hachette UK Company
www.hachette.co.uk

First published in Great Britain
in 2015 by Mitchell Beazley,
a division of Octopus Publishing
Group Ltd
Carmelite House, 50 Victoria
Embankment, London EC4Y 0DZ
www.octopusbooks.co.uk

Text copyright © Gizzi Erskine 2015
Design & layout copyright © Octopus
Publishing Group Ltd 2015
Photography copyright © The
Gaztronome 2015

ISBN 978 1 84533 963 0

A CIP catalogue record for this book
is available from the British
Library.

Printed and bound in Slovenia

10 9 8 7 6 5 4 3 2 1

Publishing Director
   Stephanie Jackson
Managing Editor Sybella Stephens
Copy Editor Clare Churly
Creative Director Jonathan Christie
Art Director & Illustrator
   Dean Martin
Designer Jaz Bahra
Photographer The Gaztronome
Home Economists Sofia Johansson,
   Anna Jones, Emily Ezekiel,
   Kat Mead
Prop Stylists Anna Jones,
   Emily Ezekiel, Linda Berlin
Senior Production Manager Peter Hunt

Firstly I need to thank everyone at Octopus. This starts with the powerhouse that is Stephanie Jackson. Thank you for investing in me. I know I'm a skittish, too busy with a distracted ADHD brain, but also a know-it-all, control freak and this is mostly a nightmare, but thank you for baring with me. I hope, like me, you think its all been worth it. To Sybella my brilliant editor whose meticulous eye, tremendous relationship with the English language and calmness has rounded this book into something so very readable. Also thanks to Pete in Production, Kevin and Stuart in Sales and Caroline in Publicity.

The design team starting with Jonathan Christie, Creative Director, for being able to help me keep my image, but ease me into growing up. Also thanks to Jaz at Octopus.
To the love of my life Dean Martin, you know me inside out and our books always capture this. Your illustrations and graphic design are exemplary; I wish you knew how good you are…
Gaz (The Gaztranomme) we knew we were taking a risk, this being your first book and all, but it paid off, the images are a beaut and never before has a photographer been more laid back.

The food team, starting with Sofia Johansson my sidekick. My God, no one has put up with more from me over this period (even Dean). You are not only a wonderful chef and sounding board for work, but my shrink, life coach and exercise buddy. WE achieve all this stuff! Not just me! Shopping for and helping me with the testing of the recipes, THEN organising me is quite a job! The home ecs, but also brilliant food writers in their own right: Anna Jones and Emily Ezekiel – I'm still reeling that you said yes! How funny was it! I still keep gaffawing at the fun we had AND you did all the outstanding propping. I hope you're as proud of the book as I am! Thanks also to Rob and Kat.

Team Gizzi: Severine Berman, my manager and soul sister – I love you like family. The rest of the gang at Roar Global, but most notably Kate, Ed and Jonathan Shalit. Tim Beaumont, my trusty PR and long time best boy pal, as always it's terrific to work with someone who is so with me in my idea of pushing the boundaries of food and PR.

To Mark, Sarah, Frankie, Olly and Laurel at *The Sunday Times Magazine* for giving me the most incredible 2 years of my life – I never believed any of this would happen for me but working with you on my column has been the absolute dream scenario.

To my mother, Maria, Spain was ACE but I couldn't have done it without you and our epic food shops and testing days. My sisters, Heni and Cora, you are my rocks, always, and Edie and Sholto for simply being Rad and a constant inspiration and keeping me sane. To Matt and Kieron, to Zoe, Martha, Elly and Rosie, Thomas Blythe. And finally to all the people who have helped me in my career. I can't name you all, but you know who you are and I owe you the world. THANK YOU! Now lets eat!